Infobesity

Infobesity

How to Be Followers of Jesus in
an Information Overload World

Andy Gabruch

FOREWORD BY
Leonard Sweet

CASCADE *Books* • Eugene, Oregon

INFOBESITY
How to Be Followers of Jesus in an Information Overload World

Copyright © 2024 Andy Gabruch. All rights reserved. Except for brief quotations in critical publications or reviews, no part of this book may be reproduced in any manner without prior written permission from the publisher. Write: Permissions, Wipf and Stock Publishers, 199 W. 8th Ave., Suite 3, Eugene, OR 97401.

Cascade Books
An Imprint of Wipf and Stock Publishers
199 W. 8th Ave., Suite 3
Eugene, OR 97401

www.wipfandstock.com

PAPERBACK ISBN: 978-1-6667-7452-8
HARDCOVER ISBN: 978-1-6667-7453-5
EBOOK ISBN: 978-1-6667-7454-2

Cataloguing-in-Publication data:

Names: Gabruch, Andy, author. | Sweet, Leonard, foreword.
Title: Infobesity : how to be followers of Jesus in an information overload world / by Andy Gabruch ; foreword by Leonard Sweet.
Description: Eugene, OR: Cascade Books, 2024 | Includes bibliographical references.
Identifiers: ISBN 978-1-6667-7452-8 (paperback) | ISBN 978-1-6667-7453-5 (hardcover) | ISBN 978-1-6667-7454-2 (ebook)
Subjects: LCSH: Discipling (Christianity) | Technology—Religious aspects—Christianity | Social media—Religious aspects—Christianity
Classification: BV4520 .G25 2024 (paperback) | BV4520 .G25 (ebook)

VERSION NUMBER 12/10/24

For Dad. With Dad.

"Whatever you do, do it all for the glory of God."
(1 Cor 10:31)

Contents

Foreword by Leonard Sweet | ix
Preface | xi
Acknowledgments | xiii
Introduction | xv

Part One: **Jesus and Infobesity**

CHAPTER ONE: Me, My Selfie, and I | 1
CHAPTER TWO: The Digital Trinity | 18
CHAPTER THREE: The Digital Garden | 32
CHAPTER FOUR: The Ancient Selfie | 42
CHAPTER FIVE: Symptoms of Infobesity | 54

Part Two: **Responding to Infobesity as Followers of Jesus**

CHAPTER SIX: Well-Being in an Infobesity World | 81
CHAPTER SEVEN: Jesus in an Infobesity World | 91
CHAPTER EIGHT: Truth as a Person in a Post-Truth World | 103
CHAPTER NINE: Community in an Infobesity World | 111

Part Three: **Redeeming Digital Spaces**

CHAPTER TEN: The Digital Practices of Jesus | 141
CHAPTER ELEVEN: Building a Jesus Brand for the Digital World to See | 150

Conclusion | 164

CONTENTS

Resources
    Infobesity Resources for Parents | 169
    Infobesity Resources for Students | 177
    Infobesity Resources for Pastors and Leaders | 182
    Infobesity 30-Day Personal Challenge | 186
    Technological "Way of Life" for Individual Template | 191
    Technological "Way of Life" for Families Template | 192
    Sample *Infobesity* Self-Assessment Infographic | 193
    Infobesity Self-Assessment Login Access | 195

Bibliography | 197

Foreword

Some words are great singly, but put together spell disaster. Like holiday cruise or avid golfer or root canal or power outage or delayed flight, or for some people, public speaking.

But many of the worst two words in the English language now come from the world of information technology. How about information overload, information leak, system update, password reset, endless scroll, influencer expertise (my personal favorite), digital wellness. But maybe the worst two words in the English language are the ones coined in this book: infobesity.

What makes our current moment unique isn't just the volume of information, but a fundamental shift in how we acquire and process it. For the first time in human history, our children don't need authority figures to access information. The traditional "big-jug-little-mug" model of education—where teachers pour knowledge into passive students—has been disrupted by smartphones that can answer any factual question in seconds.

But this ease of *access* has created a different and more urgent need: our children desperately need guides to help them *process* this torrent of information, to *assess* the difference beetween digital nutrition and digital junk food. They need mentors who can help them transform raw information into genuine knowledge, and knowledge into wisdom.

In fact, they need authority figures more than ever—not as gatekeepers of information, but as trusted guides who can help them navigate through the digital wilderness of competing claims and counterclaims, teaching them to recognize what information can be trusted and what should be treated as litter and clutter. The world of education must move from teaching as ACCESS to teaching as PROCESS and ASSESS.

Dr. Andy Gabruch has written a timely and essential guide for navigating this age of information overconsumption. Drawing on extensive research and pastoral experience, he diagnoses the symptoms of our collective infobesity and, more importantly, prescribes a healthy digital diet based on the wisdom of Jesus. This isn't just another book lamenting technology or calling for digital abstinence. Instead, it offers a balanced and biblical approach to thriving spiritually in our connected world.

What makes this book especially valuable is its practical focus on redemption rather than rejection of digital spaces. Dr. Gabruch shows us how to move from being shaped by the "digital trinity" of endless connections, consumption, and clicks to being transformed by the Holy Trinity. He helps us understand how to build what he calls a "Jesus brand" online—not for self-promotion, but for authentic Christian witness in digital spaces.

For parents trying to guide children through social media, for pastors seeking to shepherd congregations in a digital age, for anyone feeling overwhelmed by the endless stream of information—this book offers hope and practical wisdom. It reminds us that even in our digital Babylon, we can learn to be faithful exiles who bring the light of Christ into every space we occupy—including the digital ones.

The choice before us isn't whether to engage with digital spaces, but how to do so redemptively. This book will help you make that choice wisely. Read it thoughtfully, apply it practically, and share it generously. Your digital life—and your spiritual life—will be better for it.

Leonard Sweet

Author of over seventy books and Distinguished Senior Professor at Drew University, George Fox University, Southeastern University, and Northwind Seminary

Preface

The findings of *infobesity* have been a ten-year journey.

At the time, I was the Next Generation Director for the Pentecostal Assemblies of Canada, travelling the globe to train, teach, and mentor younger pastors who were keenly aware of how the rise of digital information, access to different forms of information, and the increase of digital spaces affected younger generations, their well-being, and their faith.

Due to this, I have researched, taught, and discipled countless places and spaces to help modern-day technological followers of Jesus thrive, not just survive, in an infobese world.

Then, COVID hit.

In a matter of moments, our world has become digitalized (whether you like it or not). It was not just younger generations wrestling through the plethora of *infobesity* online but all generations.

During the pandemic, I started my doctoral journey with *George Fox University*. I was focused on a rigorous pursuit of determining how followers of Jesus can increase their well-being and witness in digital spaces rather than experience the many forms of *infobesity* expressed throughout this book.

Therefore, this project aims to be a prophetic resource for you, your church, or your family.

What I mean by prophetic is providing life-giving resources to "redeem the times"—to redeem digital spaces, the church living in a digital age, and families who have become digitalized due to the latest worldwide pandemic.

As we see throughout the pages of Scripture, God would provide prophetic utterances to His people as warnings, blessings, reminders, and promises of what was, what is, and what is yet to come. Prophetic language spoke to the heart of the matter for the people of God in any given cultural or community situation.

The goal of this book is to do the same.

May you and I "redeem the times" in an *infobesity* world.

Andy Gabruch

www.infobesity.ca

Acknowledgments

I have realized it takes a committed and intentional community to reach the conclusions from this project. I am deeply grateful for the community of stakeholders, including Devan Sylvester, Cynthia Enns, and Laura O'Rilley, who have faithfully walked alongside the research. Thank you to the organizations for allowing me to partner with you on the findings from this book. I am deeply grateful for Summit Pacific College, Canadian Youth Workers Conference, Truth Matters Ministry, University Christian Ministries, the Pentecostal Assemblies of Canada, and the Evangelical Fellowship of Canada. Thank you!

To my family, who have sharpened me along the way, my wonderful partner in life, Annick Gabruch, and my children, who have walked alongside me during this journey. It has been a great one!

Of course, the investment stakeholders of Broadway Church in Vancouver, British Columbia, and my late father, Alvin Gabruch, who believed in me and my research project before I reached any of the conclusions from the research. Thank you! Words do not go far enough.

For God be the glory.

Introduction

> "Buy the Truth and do not sell it."
> —Prov 23:23

> "Don't become so well-adjusted to your culture that you fit into it without even thinking. Instead, fix your attention on God."
> —Rom 12:2 (Peterson, *Message*)

When was the last time you asked yourself, "How many hours do I spend online?"

What am I watching?

Who am I following?

What are my digital habits?

Am I distracted from key relationships in my life? Or from my work? Or in my education?

Have you ever asked these questions?

Whether you are a teacher, construction worker, pastor, student, or a stay-at-home parent, we have all experienced being distracted from living in a digital world.

We scroll, game, and have endless digital content for entertainment. It is like we are unable to turn off our digital devices.

In fact, feel free to grab your digital device. Go to your settings. Head to your screen time.

What do you see?

If you can, click on "activity." What do your digital practices reveal about you?

What is your first category of activity? Is it social media platforms? Is it your texting apps?

What is grabbing your attention the most?

Whether at work or school or with friends and family, the digital connections from our devices beg for our attention. And based on our digital practices and habits, the digital age is shaping us more than you know.

From the world shutting down because of a worldwide pandemic to schools suddenly becoming digital, the world has experienced the impact of being online like never before.

Terms like "brain fog" and "screen fatigue" and "death scrolls" have become the norm.

Our work suddenly went online. Our social media practices increased. Face-to-face conversations with loved ones moved to FaceTime connections.

We had to become digitalized in a matter of moments.

I will personally never forget it.

In my household, I remember when our world turned digital in a moment. The digital world became the primary tool for education, connecting with family and friends, and engaging us when stuck at home.

I will never forget when my wife and I were setting up four different homeschool stations with four other digital devices to help our children shift from education, from being on-site with their teachers and friends to being online.

To be honest, it was organized chaos in our home. Four stations, four other digital devices, and four classrooms are happening in the same house!

INTRODUCTION

So, naturally, our home became digital. We added the latest digital devices, increased our network, and worked, played, learned, and communicated online from our house. And, to some extent, I am thankful for this.

We bought digital devices for our children.

We became digitalized in less than twenty-four hours.

Brain fog and screen fatigue became real as we became digital teachers and parents overnight.

Working alongside our children to help them engage in their online learning was a challenge. We were teachers, parents, chefs, and employees all at the same time. And to add to all this, there were no places to go—no gym, no community, no church.

How about you? Did your home become digitalized in the matter of moments?

I am thankful for my kids being connected digitally to their education, friends, and family. I am grateful for their teachers to find creative ways to engage with our children online. I am thankful we were able to do life with my family through the challenges of becoming isolated during a modern-day pandemic.

And yet, I am not.

Fast forward to a post-pandemic world, and we are distracted (and perhaps addicted) to our digital devices like never before.

No joke, my kids have forgotten their lunches, chore lists, and the most important meal of the day (breakfast) because they are scrolling on their digital devices. School assignments have been late or rushed or extended because of gaming, communicating, or being entertained online for too long.

For consequences with our children, the number one power grab for us as parents is to take their digital devices away. And even though we continually moderate their digital consumption, it is an ongoing struggle to keep them from becoming digital zombies.

Your household may have experienced the same thing.

According to the latest research, our digital consumption has doubled since COVID.[1] Before COVID, our digital consumption was approximately three to four hours a day. That means, the average person was scrolling, snapping, gaming, or texting three to four hours a day.[2]

Since COVID, the average digital consumption is between five to six hours per day and increasing.[3]

What is complex with digital consumption is our digital practices and habits are increasing, not decreasing.

We are always connected.

It doesn't matter how many hours we are consuming digital content; we are always online.

It is true, isn't it?

We are invited to engage the digital world anytime we want.

Social media feeds, apps, and the largest tech companies design digital spaces for you and me to consume anytime at any place.

So much so that digital users have confessed being continually online because of FOMO—fear of missing out. They genuinely feel anxious if they are not online *or* not in arm's reach from their digital device. They fear not tapping fast enough on their latest notification. They fear missing out on the newest newsreel or viral video or gossip post or social activity with their digital friends or family.

In fact, according to Pew Research Center, 91 percent of us are an arm's reach away from our digital device twenty-four hours a day.[4]

We are always online.

---

1. Brandon, "New Survey."
2. Digital consumption, as I define it, is usage of social media, gaming, or any other form of digital entertainment. This does not include education and/or working on online platforms.
3. Brandon, "New Survey," para. 2.
4. Gandolf, "24/7 Dependence," para. 5.

In our research, most people experience FOMO because they fear missing what is called social information. Social information is information shared on our social media platforms designed to keep us connected with one another.

My grandma loves her social media platforms. For this reason alone, she can stay connected to her grandkids' activities, pictures, and birthdays. For her, social information gives her joy.

I would agree with grandma (grandmas are the best)!

Even though she has experienced the positive outcomes of social information, the extremes of digital usage is experiencing fear, social anxiety, and depression with a connection to FOMO.

It is real.

Many people who have consumed enormous amounts of social information have had a negative well-being experience rather than a positive one, like my grandma.

Another reality of digital usage is the ongoing concerns arising with adolescents. Even though my grandma is on her social media platforms primarily to stay connected with her family, adolescents are on social media platforms for different reasons. According to the current research, young people continue to wrestle with mental health issues linked to their digital habits.

Unfortunately, as digital spaces are not government regulated or internally moderated by any sorts of ethics like gambling, sexuality, smoking, or drug usage, the largest social media companies are enabled to manipulate their business strategies based on the vulnerabilities of young people using social information.

According to one giant tech company, their digital creators confessed to using their digital information as "peer pressure generated by the visually focused app [which] led to mental-health and body-image problems, and in some cases, eating disorders and suicidal thoughts."[5]

---

5. Associated Press, "US Senators Grill Facebook Exec," para. 7.

In addition to this, the largest social media platforms have repeatedly and personally thwarted initiatives meant to improve the well-being of teenagers, even overruling senior team members towards their own business practices.

How heartbreaking!

How toxic.

For all the world to see, digital companies are exploiting younger digital users for their profit and gain. Platforms become addictive—apps designed to be interactive and social become toxic and manipulative.

As you would already be aware, and yet it is important to repeat, giant digital tech companies release online information as a strategy to sell products, platforms, and even people based on the digital practices of their users. Algorithms are personal digital intelligence marketing tactics to grab your attention. They calculate a product for you to consume by the information you engage with by a series of quick clicks in digital spaces.

Experts call this business strategy the attention economy.

The attention economy is the practice of capturing digital users through what is known as online engagement. Online engagement may include age or stage of life, combining digital practices and habits with our digital devices to shock and awe us with digital content, including hateful and hurtful information.

It is interesting to observe, as Catherine Price has written on the attention economy and as an award-winning journalist, the link between the invention of the digital device and a 30 percent increase of mental health issues in younger generations.[6] Since COVID, mental health issues have doubled.[7] The attention economy has escalated the overwhelming amount of hateful and hurtful information online.

But this is not just the reality with adolescents. We see the damaging consequences of modern-day digital information with adults and parents alike.

---

6. Price, *How to Break Up with Your Phone*, 6.

7. Digital practices connected to isolationism. See Price, *How to Break Up with Your Phone*, 11–12.

Hateful information has included political polarization, personalized modes of truth, secret social media platforms, and constant digital distractions from always being online. The growing gaps of mistrust, skepticism, and fear in our world has increased since we have become digitalized.

Overall, I call this digital phenomenon *infobesity*. In short, *infobesity* is the symptoms of experiencing information overload from digital technologies. And since our digital device is only an arm's length away from us,[8] we have all experienced some level of *infobesity*.

In agreement, psychologist Dr. Dunkley has termed *infobesity* as ESS—electronic screen syndrome.[9] The World Health Organization has classified ESS, also known as internet addiction, as an ongoing health issue for humanity.[10] And yet, ESS is not recognized as a disorder amongst digital users in North America.

You might be skeptical reading this and say to yourself, "So what?" or, "I don't care about my digital practices. I know how to handle *infobesity*," or, "Yeah, you're right. I might be addicted, but I'm godly."

Whatever your reaction, this book is about how to redeem digital practices as followers of Jesus. We are not to react as digital users with minimal reflection or reject digital spaces outrightly but to redeem the digital world we interact with daily.

The first section of this book is designed to help you discover digital awareness. This is the ability to become aware of your personalized digital practices and habits.

Like it or not, your digital practices and habits are shaping you positively and negatively. Whether you are online for a few moments, ten hours a day, or twenty-five hours a day, your digital consumption reveals something more profound about you. If you are unaware of your digital practices and habits, you will intentionally or unintentionally allow the digital world to shape you negatively. The symptoms of *infobesity* in your digital

---

8. According to post by Dave Adamson (@aussiedave), author of *MetaChurch*, 91 percent of adults keep their smartphones within arm's reach all day (X, December 21, 2022, 3:50 PM).
9. DeFrank, *Digital Detox*, 30.
10. Korte, "Impact of the Digital Revolution," para. 4.

spaces can have harmful effects on your well-being, key relationships, and even on your outlook on life.

As we are designed to be social creatures, the highest form of learning is personal. We lead by example.

Whether we are parents, a teacher, a construction worker, a pastor, a leader of an organization or business, or students, the highest form of learning is to lead by example.

Josh McDowell once said, "Rules without relationship leads to rebellion." I would agree with his words.

We cannot overcome the symptoms of *infobesity* in our homes, businesses, or churches unless we are self-aware enough to regulate our digital practices and habits.

As you read through these pages, an *infobesity* self-assessment will be available. This assessment will help you understand your digital practices, develop healthy digital habits, and provide opportunities to redeem our digital world.

The second section of this book is designed to empower and teach digital users how to respond to digital practices and habits as a follower of Jesus. As digital disciples, have you ever asked yourself how Jesus impacts your digital consumption?

If I was honest, my grandma didn't ask these questions either! She just wanted to see pictures of her grandkids. Yet, when her digital practices and habits increased over time, her social media platforms were littered with misinformation and disinformation. From political posts to religious nonsense, her feeds became more harmful than helpful.

As her grandkids, we had to help her regulate her ESS—*infobesity* symptoms—as she had to filter through the information she was being bombarded with.

In fact, I didn't ask this question in my life until I went through the research. Would Jesus care about what or why or where or when I was online? Is there any merit to what it means to be a disciple of Jesus in a digital age?

INTRODUCTION

This is why we developed the *infobesity* self-assessment. It allows digital users to understand, regulate, moderate, and redeem digital practices and habits in practical ways as followers of Jesus.

Too often, I have experienced followers of Jesus either rejecting digital spaces and not engaging in the digital world altogether or followers of Jesus receiving digital spaces with limited personal reflection at all. It is like Jesus never lived in their digital spaces.

Too often, great people who love Jesus and live Christlike lives in the real world have become too naïve to their digital practices. They have fallen prey to *infobesity* and have not represented Jesus well.

We can all agree this has happened to all of us at some point in our digital lives.

The book's third part is the most important as followers of Jesus. We will explore how to equip you, your home, church, and business or organization to redeem digital spaces. As followers of Jesus, he allows us to bring glory to God in every area of life, including our digital practices and spaces.

The apostle Paul, an early church leader, wrote to the people of God in the ancient city of Corinth. The Corinthians were known as a secular, oversexualized, and individualistic culture. To encourage them, their pastor challenged them to glorify God with their daily practices in everyday life. He put it this way: "So whether you eat or drink or whatever you do, do it *all* for the glory of God" (1 Cor 10:31).

The same encouragement remains for us today.

In a digital—a secular, oversexualized, and individualistic—world, this book empowers followers of Jesus on how to bring glory to God in all we do.

As you may already know, the digital age is here to stay. The question—and the opportunity—is to be aware of our digital practices, be empowered by Jesus to respond to our digital habits, and know how to redeem digital spaces as disciples of Jesus.

Whether you are a teacher, construction worker, pastor, student, or stay-at-home parent, I encourage you to engage in the practical actions and attitudes of how to be a follower of Jesus as you are living, breathing, working, communicating, and trying to follow Jesus in an *infobesity* world.

Personal Reflections

- How much time do you spend on digital consumption? Share your digital activity with someone according to your digital device settings.
- Have you experienced modern-day *infobesity*? What symptoms have you experienced?
- Out of the different forms of social, hurtful, or harmful information, what type of information do you tend to engage with the most?
- How can you redeem the symptoms of *infobesity* you're facing as a follower of Jesus?

PART ONE: **Jesus and Infobesity**

CHAPTER ONE: Me, My Selfie, and I

"The one who shares the best story wins."
—Leonard Sweet

"Protect your heart for it is the wellspring of life."
—King Solomon

We live in a selfie world, don't we?

Interestingly, 2.4 billion pictures are taken with digital devices daily (and growing). Of the 2.4 billion images taken daily, 92 million are selfies. A selfie is a self-taken photo from a digital device (like a smartphone).[1] Each day, digital users average seven minutes taking selfies.[2]

In conversation with a few friends, one of our friends began bragging about how many photos she had on her smartphone. She asked us to guess how many pictures she had on her digital device. Someone mentioned, "Five thousand photos." She shook her head, confessing, "Higher." Another person shouted out, "Eight thousand photos." Our friend laughed and said, "Nope! Higher." We all began to laugh with her, and I finally blurted out, "Twenty-thousand photos." She said, "Seventeen thousand," with a gasp, and then said, "I have over ten thousand selfies!"

She had the most photos I have ever heard of on a smartphone. I don't know how much storage she needs to have so many images, but she ended

---

1. Wikipedia, "Selfie," https://en.wikipedia.org/wiki/Selfie.
2. Broz, "Selfie Statistics."

the dialogue by saying, "You can judge me all you want if I take too many photos, but my selfies make me happy!"

If we are honest with ourselves, my friend is right, isn't she? We take photos of everything! Why? Because taking pictures of ourselves, our moments, our memories makes us happy!

We take photos of our breakfast. We take selfies with the sunset. We take pictures with our friends. We take a selfie on a beach. We share photos of our random yet meaningful experiences.

Typically, though, we snap selfies of what makes us happy. Our selfies make us look good. We share selfies with the digital world because we feel good about ourselves. And when we don't feel happy about ourselves, there are apps to filter us to appear cool or attractive or make us look better than we do.

The modern-day selfie world is how we want to be seen by the world. Humanly speaking, we all want to be known by the world. We all want to belong to something or someone. We want to be cheered on by those who love us. We want to be celebrated by others. We want to be affirmed, even with strangers.

Social platforms and spaces have allowed this human need to be recognized and manipulated. For example, local musicians, actors, and influencers succeed enormously through their selfies. But it isn't just musicians, actors, or influencers who do this; we all do! We all want to be accepted to be digitally famous.

Even in my own home, my kids are not motivated to be a firefighter or a police officer. They are not interested in becoming an astronaut. They want to be an online influencer making buckets of cash! Yet, the more profound human desire is to be seen, heard, and celebrated; and if we are not, we are met with ongoing disappointment at the very core of our being.

The likes, the pings, and the dings on our selfie culture lures you and me to increase our online engagement and frequency. There is even an International Selfie Day.[3] Yes, we live in a world that likes to celebrate ourselves. It is like we live for ourselves and within ourselves through a selfie world.

---

3. See "International Selfie Day."

CHAPTER ONE: ME, MY SELFIE, AND I

According to an online guru named Dave Adamson, who wrote a book called *MetaChurch*, younger generations are spending approximately 7.3 hours per day online.[4] The access to unlimited information, the abundance of digital platforms, and personalization of digital spaces (based on our distinctive digital habits and practices) are increasing our digital consumption in our selfie culture.

Due to the selfie world we live in, we are more connected to each other than ever before. In moments, we can text, snap, messenger, chat, FaceTime, Zoom, email, emoji, anything, anywhere, at any time. Yet, we are profoundly disconnecting from one another.[5]

According to psychologist Henry Cloud, the rise of the selfie in digital spaces has stunted the ability to develop meaningful relationships with each other.[6] We unthinkingly focus on relationships based on the selfie culture of our needs and wants, and because we live like our selfies, we lose the ability to form meaningful relationships. In any meaningful relationship, connectedness is encouraged through intentional expressions of community. You cannot have a thriving relationship with self-serving desires. Hence the rise of modern-day loneliness.[7]

Not only does the digital age want to keep you connected at all times, but it also intends to keep you informed about everything (and nothing) simultaneously.

As human beings, not only do we desire to be celebrated, wanted, loved, and appreciated in meaningful relationships, we want to make a difference in this world. For this to happen, we need to know what is happening in our world.

Digital companies know this.

---

4. Adamson, *MetaChurch*, 33.

5. We discuss the effects of modern-day loneliness, isolationism, and how to combat loneliness in chapter 8.

6. Henry Cloud (@DrHenryCloud), "Love may come naturally, but that doesn't mean that it can't leave us feeling uncertain and inadequate. Despite our efforts, we may struggle to maintain strong relationships in various areas of our lives, including parenting, marriage, friendship, and even business" (X, January 4, 2023, 7:10 AM).

7. We will go in-depth on the concept of modern-day loneliness in chapter 5.

PART ONE: JESUS AND INFOBESITY

In addition to FOMO, the invention of the "like" on our social media platforms and "pings" from our digital devices, and the "hearts" on our posts are numerous ways big tech companies want to captivate us with the latest and instantaneous information existing in digital spaces.[8] These spaces keep us connected to what is going on around us so with the lure of wanting to make a difference in these spaces. But the buzzes of our digital devices distract us enough and offer minor dopamine hits to keep us engaged and interactive in the content flung at us rather than making a difference around us.

A great example of this is the ongoing issue of texting and driving.

In my area of the world, texting and driving causes more accidents than any other form of distracted driving, including driving under the influence of alcohol and drugs. Insurance premiums have increased over 30 percent, and texting while driving fines have tripled.

How is texting and driving so dangerous? It is because the digital buzzes, dings, bings, and rings from our handheld devices calling out to us to respond instantly, trigger dopamine hits to our brains to keep us happy. Hence, this is why we text and drive. We want to remain connected. We want to eagerly stay informed through our digital devices. Not only is our digital consumption increasing because of the plethora of connections or fostered FOMO or exploiting the likes and pings from your digital device, but also because the digital age wants to engage you through a series of quick algorithmic clicks.

Whether you know it (or like it) or not, the digital age shapes you. These spaces and places shape you based on your online clicks. Your preferences, digital habits, and practices reveal information about you. These clicks (and snaps) shape how you communicate, foster relationships, interact with work, and see the world. The digital age is personalized around you.

For me, I engage in quick clicks to find direct answers. With just a few clicks online, I can fix minor issues with my car, connect with family, interact with friends, work on my business, pay bills, buy and sell items, and so much more! With a few clicks and links on my smartphone, it is truly unique, helpful, and lightning-fast to find what information I am are looking for.

8. Vega, "Sean Parker on Facebook."

If I have a question about anything, I can access enormous amounts of information in moments from my fingertips. And yet, with all the positives the digital world grants you and me, the digital age can overwhelm us with excessive information.

Scientists from Temple University have indicated that when digital users experienced too much information online, their prefrontal cortexes simply shut down.[9]

This is why irritability, anger, and frustration rises with moderate to heavy internet usage.[10] The ability to focus on meaningful work or relationships decreases. Developing healthy coping skills or self-awareness techniques toward common sense simply shuts down. The brain canal disengages from access to too much information.

It is like we become brain-numbed digital zombies.

The science behind digital zombies is substantial. For example, as parents, we recognized the symptoms of digital zombies as our children interact with the digital world during the pandemic. In my home, my wife and I termed my kid's irritability, irrational fits of anger, and lack of relational awareness as "COVID kids." In agreeance, talking to a local school principal, he mentioned isolationism and digital interaction in younger generations during COVID have caused extra work for his elementary school staff. The lack of retention of learning, fear of peer social interactions, and lack of classroom respect has had to be addressed in the classroom (and at home). Maybe as a parents you have experienced the same.

As the pandemic has eased, we have become increasingly aware of the digital symptoms our family is facing. Psychologist Malcolm Gladwell echoes this modern-day information overload and *infobesity* as channel capacity.[11] It is the area of the brain which processes information; and as human beings, we can only process so much information.

Unchecked information overload causes delusional experiences. Brain fatigue sets in. If not addressed, information overload can increase fits of

---

9. Vaughan, "Know Your Limits," para. 2.
10. Price, *How to Break Up with Your Phone*, 10–11.
11. Gladwell, *Tipping Point*, 175.

anger, rage, hate, and polarization over screens. These mental indicators from information overload added to my research on *infobesity*.

Infobesity, as we will discuss in this book, is a series of symptoms of information overload experienced in digital spaces and places. As you will discover, the level of *infobesity* you and I are experiencing is connected to our purpose in this world. Everyone who engages in digital spaces and places will wrestle with various symptoms of infobesity.

As a Canadian, I love watching hockey. Growing up, I loved hockey so much that I would play hockey at school, at home in the garage, at the pond during the winters, in hallways at church, and even in our home's basement. I love hockey! Hockey is life in Canada (even if you don't understand it). If you live in Canada, you watch, play, or talk about hockey.

In one of the most prestigious hockey tournaments in the world, one of the up-and-coming best Canadian hockey players in the world confessed to his struggle with *infobesity*. His name is Conner McDavid. He was sixteen years old at the time.

Considered the best player at this prestigious tournament, he confessed how his social media practices during the tournament caused him to be distracted. His symptoms of *infobesity* caused him to not be at his best when he was on the ice.

His digital practices fueled frustration. He underperformed at games. Consequently, his team came in second at the tournament (even though they were the favorites to win the tournament). McDavid was devastated. So was the team. So was Canada!

The following year, however, as the team captain, he challenged his teammates to stay off social media during the tournament.

Why?

So they could focus on winning.

Notably, the team played exceptionally well. They were focused. They gelled as a team. They were nimble and adjusted their play when needed. They were a well-oiled machine, as a Canadian hockey team is meant to be. They played at their very best.

And guess what! They swept the competition with hockey mastery! I was proud to be a Canadian when they won the coveted gold medal at the World Juniors tournament.[12]

Now, if you ask Connor McDavid if limiting his social media during the World Juniors was the deciding factor in winning gold in 2015, he would not be able to give a defining answer.

That said, though, it points out what can happen when we are aware of the negative effects of our digital habits. The lesson from McDavid? We can be at our best when we regulate our digital consumption.

When we regulate our digital consumption, we can focus on what is essential. When we are aware of our digital practices, we can become agile and flexible to meet the demands of everyday life. When we understand our symptoms of *infobesity*, we can adjust and live in purpose, meaning, and significance; knowing our connection with the divine is more important than the digital.

I think Connor McDavid would have the same advice for us, too. Fast-forward six years later, Connor McDavid, who is arguably the best hockey player in the NHL, told Connor Bedard (who is an up-and-coming hockey star in the NHL), as the captain of Team Canada at the World Juniors in 2021, to "stay off of social media."[13]

Why would McDavid give this advice to Bedard? It is simple. Digital practices affect us—positively and negatively.

Digital practices, especially around social media, have progressively had adverse effects on our well-being. In our research, we have observed for every hour of digital usage, 1 percentage point decreases the well-being of digital users. Confessed anxiety, stress, depression, physical comparison, and feelings of unhappiness and self-destructive thoughts increase with higher levels of digital consumption.[14]

---

12. Wikipedia, "2015 World Junior Ice Hockey Championships," https://en.wikipedia.org/wiki/2015_World_Junior_Ice_Hockey_Championships.

13. TSN pre-competitive game between Canada vs. Russia, December 23, 2021 (7:54 in the 3rd period).

14. Haidt et al., "Social Media and Mental Health," 110.

Just like selfies on social media platforms, more people have died from attempting extreme selfies than from shark attacks.[15] Think about this for a moment: people have physically died from *infobesity*.[16]

This is sad.

Unmoderated and unregulated digital habits and practices steal people from their life purpose.

Whether being distracted from our best, like Connor McDavid, or searching for the next extreme selfie for the world to celebrate us, we can be negatively influenced by the digital world.

In the early 2000s, tech engineers developed a brilliant idea to handle the negative aspects of *infobesity*. They decided to filter online information through algorithms.

What are algorithms, you ask?

Simply put, algorithms filter through massive amounts of information for digital users. These digital processes are determined by the online habits, location, and practices of you and I. Massive artificial intelligent computers are programming and shifting through our online habits to match digital information to our preferences, wants, and desires.

Furthermore, algorithms, by design, share, like, and consume information sponsored or advertised by companies. Personalized information is meant to mold to our digital practices and habits to keep us further engaged online. This could include fake bots, social information you and I enjoy, and even hurtful information social sciences use to grab at our attention economy. This is presented to you and me to continuously click on their product or service or experience.[17] Digital spaces are not just designed to share information but to buy your information. Due to this, the problem of *infobesity* remains. Because algorithms are designed around your online consumption, preferences, and selfies rather than information leading to truth, we can conclude not all information is created equal, is it?

---

15. AFP, "Selfies Kill More People than Shark Attacks."
16. Güell, "Rise of Selfie Deaths."
17. Jones, *From Social Media to Social Ministry*, 54.

In fact, large amounts of *infobesity* are simply feeding into our own selfishness and biases rather than leading us to the Savior.

Just like the lady who has thousands of selfies on her digital device or Connor McDavid not being at his hockey best, digital spaces are meant to distract us, interact with us, engage our preferences, and entertain us with information that is personalized and developed by the platform to keep us happy.

I call this algorithmic authority.

It is when technology is manipulating our online information based on our attention economy practices. As mentioned before, attention economy is the cognitive reasoning designed to convinced us to spend most of our time online. This can include our recent likes on social platforms, or Google searches, or the latest product pursuits. Due to this, our online information is tailored to our unique attention economy. Unfortunately, this leads to the problem of authority.

Now, authority is not about who or what controls your life but who or what you allow to control your life.

In a world that is shifting from abstract truths to personalized experiences through selfies, for example, we must be aware of who has the authority of our lives.

Len Sweet, a mentor of mine who is a distinguished professor at George Fox University and has written over seventy books on culture, Christ, and the church, puts it this way: "The authority of our lives is the one who is the author of our lives."[18]

This rings so true. Whoever or whatever we allow in our lives is what is writing the pages of our lives. And in a world of constant selfies and images of self, we are creating our own authorities, aren't we?

The question (or more like the challenge) is, "Who is the author of your life?"

Who is writing your story?

Is social media writing your story . . .

---

18. Len Sweet, personal communication with the author, 2021.

PART ONE: JESUS AND INFOBESITY

Is your past writing your story . . .

Is Google writing your story . . .

or . . .

Can God write your story?

The challenge is, who is the author of your story?

Is it the latest selfie or the whispers from the Savior?

Is it the latest cutting-edge social media app shaping you or the living, breathing activity from the Scriptures?

Are the pings, dings, and likes distracting you more than living on purpose with Jesus?

The most important question we need to ask ourselves in our selfie world is, "Is Jesus the author of my life or is it my selfie?"

If he is, then he has the ultimate authority in your life.

Not you.

Not your selfie.

Not your feelings.

Not your political outlook.

Not your social follower count or likes or comments.

It is Jesus.

In our modern-day digital world, we do not have a truth problem as much as an authority problem.

Even in the early church, we see the ancient followers of Jesus wrestle with the modern struggle of authority.

Followers of Jesus in the ancient city of Colossae, for example, were facing the pressures of authority. Roman culture was encouraging multiple gods to be experienced, not just the One named Jesus. Weird folk religions

CHAPTER ONE: ME, MY SELFIE, AND I

in the area bombarded people with experiences with false spirits rather than the Holy Spirit. Just like what we face online, the false information we experience today is the same false information the church faced two thousand years ago.

Furthermore, the early Christians in Colossae experienced pressure from local religious leaders. They were being bombarded with information to conform to their religious practices. If people wanted to have a proper relationship with God, they had to follow their religious authority. Based on their own selfish, yet religious ways, these leaders based a relationship with God on past rituals rather than living a mature relationship with Jesus. The early followers of Jesus were clashing with who had the ultimate authority to shape their lives.

Was it the religious leaders? Was it the false spirits of the day? Or the pressures of Roman culture?

Similarly, our modern society continues to bombard us, as digital users, to chase after experiences of the selfie culture rather than encounter the truth found in Scripture as our ultimate authority.

The apostle Paul, an early church leader, would agree. He puts it this way:

> Don't let anyone capture you with empty philosophies and high-sounding nonsense that come from human thinking and from the spiritual powers of this world, rather than from Christ. For in Christ lives all the fullness of God in a human body. So you also are complete through your union with Christ, who is the head over every ruler and authority. (Col 2:8–10 NLT)

Let's unpack this . . .

"Don't let anyone . . ."

"Anyone," obviously, includes anyone—including yourself, your selfie, and your digital platforms. In the digital age which tracks every digital practice you and I engage in, your digital consumption is included in the "anyone" Paul is writing about. He is speaking about the reality of authority. Remember, the author of your life is who or what you allow in your life. Authority is who or what is shaping your life. And in a digital age, where online consumption is increasing, your selfies may be shaping your life with symptoms of *infobesity* more than you know. Your selfie might be distracting you from meaning, purpose, and being at your best. Your selfie might be decreasing your well-being as a follower of Jesus.

Who is the authority in your life?

Furthermore, Paul continues,

"Capture you with empty philosophies and high-sounding nonsense . . ."

As you would know, there is an enormous amount of information online.

According to researchers at the University of California at Berkeley's School of Information, there is more information being produced in the last thirty years than the last five thousand years combined.[19] Experts believe the next one hundred years will create one hundred thousand years' worth of content.[20] This is truly a phenomenon; an information transfiguration[21] or an information reformation since the printing press I would say.

But not all information is the same.

As digital companies spend billions of dollars to understand your digital practices, they have digital strategies to "capture" you with information.

The term Paul used to term "capture" to the Colossians is the same as being "captive" or to be "imprisoned" or "enticed" to be "controlled"[22] by empty philosophies and high-sounding nonsense.

In the digital world, these empty philosophies and high-sounding nonsense sounds about right, doesn't it?

The internet is full of fake information. Fake information is not helpful information. It is information which hasn't been challenged or reviewed by experts or peer-based research. Fake information is considered the highest form of information in digital spaces. In a recent study by PlushCare, their medical professional team observed over five hundred videos with

---

19. Sweat, "How Can You Deal with Information Overload?," para. 8.
20. Sherwood, "Leading and Succeeding."
21. Schultze. *Habits of the High-Tech Heart*, 16.
22. "συλαγωγέω 'to gain control of by carrying off as booty, make captive of, rob τινά someone' (Tat. 22, 2 [fig.]; Heliod. 10, 35 p. 307, 32 Bekker οὗτός ἐστιν ὁ τὴν ἐμὴν θυγατέρα συλαγωγήσας; Aristaen. 2, 22 Hercher) in imagery of carrying someone away fr. the truth into the slavery of error Col 2:8" (Arndt et al., *Greek-English Lexicon*, 955).

over twenty-five million views have found their information fake, inaccurate, or damaging to their viewers.[23] This type of information tempts us to engage; desiring you and me to distract us and lure our attention into empty philosophies and high-sound nonsense. All of us can think of the ongoing examples of fake information online.

One of my favorites is from 2017. It is a fake picture of a shark swimming in Houston, Texas, after Hurricane Harvey. It didn't take much time for the picture to go viral. Hundreds of thousands of likes and shares of the photograph were cluttering the internet in a matter of days. In fact, thousands of digital users believed the fake picture to be real simply because it went viral. Based on the engagements of the post, it was later revealed to be fake by the content creator.[24] Interestingly enough, the practical joke of a phony picture of a shark swimming in downtown Houston, Texas reveals how fake information pulls at our attention.

The question, however, is how we filter through fake information. Not all digital users have a filtering system to thoughtfully discern the crazy amounts of information coming at us. As mentioned before, unfiltered and unguarded quantities of digital information causing *infobesity*, which harms our well-being and the well-being of others around us.

Due to this, we need to develop filtering systems to discern between what is fake information and helpful information. We will address this in section two and three of this book.

The internet is not only overflowing with fake information. The digital age is full of disinformation.

Disinformation is online information shared by digital users as an opinion from another digital user. It is a lie from a digital user, not truth. If I was honest, disinformation was single-handedly shaping my grandma's online practices. She has had difficulty sifting through the information blasted on her social media platforms.

Whether it was a political or contentious post or what was on her social media feeds, disinformation was engaging her.

---

23. Sood, "How to Counter TikTok," para. 14.
24. Ohlheiser, "No, the Shark Picture Isn't Real."

The same is true with you and I. We don't have to look too far to hear words like "alternate facts"[25] or "this is my truth"[26] as nonnegotiable opinions. And in a selfie world, we tend to put our own personal authority as alternate facts or my truth on our social media feeds rather than the Truth. We, too, become agents of disinformation.

How do we filter through disinformation on our social media platforms? How do we not become agents of disinformation as followers of Jesus?

For my grandma, it was the awful and painful conversations over the phone about how to discern, delete, and decide what posts should be on her social media platforms or not. In all honesty, her digital practices and habits were changing. For her, the motivation to have social media was to stay connected to her grandkids, and now, engaging in posts engineered to the contentious issues of the day, eloquently drafted as disinformation. As you and I (and my grandma) wrestle through digital information, bombarding us with fake information and disinformation, we must navigate another stream of information online. It is the interactions with misinformation.

Misinformation is information unintentionally shared by digital users we trust. This may include trusted friends and family members. It could consist of a digital influencer we have connected with. In any case, misinformation is another tactic digital companies use to gain access to our attention economy.

Interestingly enough, a social media trend in 2018 revealed information shared from personal social media platforms were 51 percent more trusted than information shared from standard social media channels.[27] Furthermore, this study revealed an eightfold increase in engagement of information from personal social media platforms than traditional branding platforms. Whether shared intentionally or unintentionally, we gravitate to believe online misinformation from people we trust.

Due to this, we can become trapped with empty philosophies and high-sounding nonsense just like the followers of Jesus were facing in ancient Colossae.

25. Wikipedia, "Alternative facts," https://en.wikipedia.org/wiki/Alternative_facts.
26. UrbanDictionary, "My Truth," https://www.urbandictionary.com/define.php?term=My%20Truth.
27. Trainers Conference, Steve Nash Fitness World, June 8, 2018.

CHAPTER ONE: ME, MY SELFIE, AND I

In addition to the amount of information blasting at you and me online, it's estimated 15 to 60 percent (and growing) of social media do not belong to real people.[28] That's right, fake platforms pretending to be real people. Computers act like real people and share fake information on our social media sites; these are known as digital bots.

Let's pause to see how much misinformation is being shared on our personal social media platforms. Have you ever thought your social media sites could be littered with followers, likes, and comments with fake digital bots?

For example, suppose you have one thousand followers online (depending on the social media platform). There could be a case that your social media platforms has up to six hundred followers are either fake bots, or real people acting fake which are not engaging with your social media content. Sounds depressing, doesn't it? I wish my followers were more engaging, but the stats make sense.

Unfortunately, tech companies create moderated fake accounts pretending to be real people. This is to increase online engagement from you and me. It could include a like or a comment on a old social media post. It could even include an online conversation with fake social media account. The reason for this is that fake social media accounts are developed to increase their own information with us. It seems like the battle with modern-day digital bots are real. We interact with fake bots every day. Due to this, to manage our digital practices and habits, we need to discern what is fake and real on our social media platforms.

Another technique social media companies use to keep you "captive" to the empty words and continuous babble is what I call hateful information.[29]

Hateful information is information designed to shock you when you are online. One giant tech company has acknowledged using hateful information techniques as a strategy to increase engagement.

As an example, according to *The Washington Post* in a series called "Facebook under fire," an internal investigation into the digital company known as Meta reveals the damaging effects of body comparison.[30] The use of

---

28. Murphy, *You're Not Listening*, 15.
29. Col 2:8 in Peterson, *Message*.
30. Lima, "Whistleblower's Power."

deepfakes,[31] filters, and computer generated images and videos have had hateful effects on digital users. Studies with younger generations, especially, have revealed people under age twenty-five are deeply vulnerable to the damaging effects of physical comparison. Even with adults and parents, the signs of *infobesity*, of the hateful information known as physical comparison, are real.

One in five young men and one in three young women have compared themselves physically to deepfakes, computer-altered images or videos, and online models. It has intentionally caused an increase in mental illness, anxiety, depression, and personal hate. Yet, the digital company defends their business practices because of profits. When this news hit the public, Meta boasted of having a five billion dollar surplus for the quarter (even though the company recognized the harmful effects of *infobesity*, especially in younger users).

In competition, digital bots have built entire businesses by sharing hateful information. This includes sexual content, boasting the use of artificial images and fake videos, revealing the overwhelming evidence of a crowded digital world with empty words and babble, to self-regulate and moderate digital information as followers of Jesus.

Friend, these are just a few examples of why we need to be able to understand our digital practices and habits as followers of Jesus in a digital age. As Christians—like the Christians in ancient Colossae—we need to be aware of the empty words and babble of fake information, disinformation, misinformation, and hateful information relentlessly designed to shape us.

As you can see, we need to "protect our hearts as it is the wellspring of life" (Prov 4:23). This includes protecting our homes, families, and businesses from the harmful effects of *infobesity*.

Personal Reflections

- What type of information do you engage with the most (fake information, disinformation, misinformation, or hateful information)? Why or why not?
- How many selfies do you take a day (across all digital spaces)?

31. Wikipedia, "Deepfake," https://en.wikipedia.org/wiki/Deepfake.

- How do you filter through information as a follower of Jesus? Share your experience at www.infobesity.ca.
- How can Jesus be the author of your story in a selfie world?

CHAPTER TWO: The Digital Trinity

"Attention is the beginning of devotion."
—MARY OLIVER

"We are what we click."
—INFOBESITY PARTICIPANT

Where do you go when you need help? Whether it is a flashing light on your car dashboard or to find a good place to eat, where do you go to search for a quick answer?

If it is me, the first place I go to is click on digital spaces. If I want to find the best reviews on a mechanic before I give my car to the mechanic or if I want to go to a great restaurant, I search digital spaces.

In fact, if I have a question about anything, I can find any answer I want in a matter of moments online. If I am struggling through something I am not happy with, I can connect with trusted friends or experts on their social media platforms. If I am looking for a great place to eat, I open up an app and read the reviews.

For me, I default to search for answers online. How about you? If we are honest with ourselves, most of us search for answers online even when it is the most important decisions to make. We click to filter through the best relationship advice. We will search for online spaces to find the best places to live or the best job to get. We will scour the internet for parenting tips. We watch videos on how to maintain our personal well-being.

CHAPTER TWO: THE DIGITAL TRINITY

Access to the internet has allowed us to research, seek, and find any type of information we want or need at any time. And this gives us the accessibility to gather knowledge and understand information on any subject or question or need with relative ease.

But, as with life, the harder the questions we ask online, the harder it is to find clarity to our answers. For example, if I type the word "leadership" in a search bar, over 1.4 billion articles, books, videos, or blogs pop up in less than a second. How is it possible to find any answers I need on leadership? Of course, I have as much information as I will ever need on the topic of leadership, but how will I filter, search, and apply the appropriate information on the topic of leadership? How will 1.4 billion searches on leadership lead to contextualized wisdom?

You see, the problem isn't amount of information we receive online or the accessibility of information on digital platforms we search, but how we process online information we consume. Without proper instruction, we are filled with the conceit of wisdom instead of real wisdom.[1]

As Jesus wisely noted, "Ask and it will be given to you; seek and you will find; knock and the door will be opened to you. For everyone who asks receives; the one who seeks finds; and to the one who knocks, the door will be opened" (Matt 7:7–8 NIV).

He knows the pursuit of humanity's conquest to seek, search, and find truth. Yet, with online information, humanity's conquest to seek, search, and find truth is based on filtering information and, perhaps, misinformed answers to our questions. As we have already discussed, online information manipulates the truth towards the business model of a digital platform.[2]

But before we respond to how we can filter online information to work towards truth and wisdom as followers of Jesus, we need to understand the functions of the digital world.

The digital world is not only designed to bombard you with information but to entertain you.

---

1. Plato, *Phaedrus and the Seventh and Eighth Letters*, 96.
2. This can include the consequences of digital technologies as mentioned above.

If you become aware of your digital habits, you will realize how the digital world wants to entertain you.

The likes, hearts, feeds, dings, notifications, and buzzes are meant to keep you entertained, not just distracted.

Videos. Scrolling. Alerts. Clicks. All are meant to keep you engaged online.

And when they do, it is easy to become unproductive and distracted from being the very best we are created to be.

So, how does the digital world entertain you?

Well, one way the digital world is designed to entertain you is to continually connect with you and I to each other. As we have discovered, this is called social information. In digital spaces, social information is for you and me to stay connected with relationships, products, programs, games, platforms, apps, social media—fill in the blank—to keep us entertained online.

In the light of entertainment, we connect with relationships—friends and strangers—who engage us with our social needs. We entertain ourselves with questions, seeking answers to our current needs, finding solutions to our programs, building paradigms for life in an increasing amount of efficiency.

With such efficiency, we have unlimited amounts of digital consumption to be entertained with any time at any place.

Even though connections online have positive effects to our overall well-being, social media experts reveal the negative symptoms of *infobesity* uniquely tied to our moderate levels of digital practices with entertainment. We are simply consumed with entertainment. Mild forms *infobesity* cause FOMO or social anxiety, incessantly engaging digital users through online connections known to be entertaining to them.

This leads to a second way the digital world entertains you and me: digital spaces and places are designed to be consumed.

Whatever your heart desires, you can consume online. The latest products, the hottest videos, the smuttiest gossip, the newest breaking news, entertaining hobbies—you and I can even consume relationships online in a matter of clicks and moments.

CHAPTER TWO: THE DIGITAL TRINITY

Modern-day psychologists call this attention theory.[3] We have discussed the attention economy; attention theory is different. Attention theory is the design behind digital platforms, where the attention economy is the information shared on these platforms. Each strategy is meant to pull your attention. These practices are meant to engage you for profitable returns. It is a hook, line, and sinker strategy for your attention. However, there is only so much attention you can give.

For instance, you and I are consuming five times more information per day than those living in the 1980s and 1990s. It is the equivalent to consuming one hundred and seventy-five newspapers per day or one hundred-thousand words of content or twenty gigabytes of information each and every day.[4] It would be the same as reading a full novel or two help-self books in a single day.

Of course, we cannot retain these enormous amounts of information with our brains.

In fact, experts suggest there will be one hundred-thousand years' worth of information in digital spaces by 2100.[5]

Due to this natural limitation, we can only retain a certain amount of information. We call this capacity information processing, and it is limited to the capacity to our human reasoning.

Information psychologists have determined human beings can retain approximately one hundred and twenty bits of information per second. This limitation, practically speaking, has an informational ceiling point. For example, humans are limited to the information retention of one conversation at a time. This is why it is extremely difficult to have a meaningful conversation with someone and watch the football game at the same time. It just cannot happen. Your brain will shift through primary and secondary modes of information based on your preference at the time. The retention of information we consume is based on the importance of information being presented to us.

---

3. Jenny Odell spends a great deal of time on how the digital age is designed to grab your attention in her book, *How to Do Nothing: Resisting the Attention Economy*.

4. Levitin, *Organized Mind*, Kindle loc. 429.

5. Sherwood, "Leading and Succeeding."

Consider this: you are at a restaurant with your significant other. Even in this simple scenario, your brain is filtering through enormous amounts of information to focus on what is important to you at any given moment.

Think about it: our brains are subconsciously limiting the information of the distractions around you to focus on the person you are having dinner with. The noises from the forks and knives pinging on the plates, the waiters or waitresses running past your table, the softly played music in the background, the conversations behind your table; you are filtering secondary information in your brain by focusing on the person across from you as primary information. Your subconscious brain is filtering through information all the time so that you can retain information that matters to you.

In the same way, your brain is filtering through hundreds of distracting "bytes" of information when you are driving. Imagine with me: as you are driving down the highway, your brain is shifting through masses of information around you, so that you can continue to stay focused on your driving skills. Your brain is selecting which information is important, and which is not important. The cars racing by, the trees alongside the road, the upcoming intersections, merging lanes, and a dozen other pieces of information being filtered by your brain each moment. The only way you will react to primary and secondary modes of information as a driver is through an alert. This could include a signal light of a car merging into your lane, and you slow down. It could mean a honked horn of a car warning you of an upcoming risk. In any case, our brains are wired to filter through information to find what is important to us at that moment.

This is what is called information theory. It suggests our brains filter through millions of bytes of information based on importance—what we truly value at the time—at any given moment.

It applies to our digital practices too. Attention theory, attention economies, and information importance are digital designs used to surprise, distract, bombard, and engage us with digital information in digital spaces. When this occurs, our brains sift through enormous amounts of online information to focus on what information will be consumed based on personal importance.

I call this entertainment information.

It is proven information which is entertaining is more likely to be consumed by digital users than any other form of information. This includes social media scrolling, meme sharing, and, for example, the unending cat videos.

And interestingly enough, the increased amounts of attention economies released online through entertainment correlates to the increased amounts of profits from digital users; and consequently, mental health concerns and decreased well-being in digital users as well.

Evidence suggests attention economy is focused on the importance and changes the brain activity in digital users. The brain manages information based on what is shocking, sexualized, hateful, or harmful to distract our attention on these forms of information in digital spaces.

We experience what McDavid experienced in the World Juniors. We are not at our best when we are digitally absorbed.

Due to the massive amounts of information we encounter, equal to a six-hundred page book per day, we typically consume online information important to us. It can include information on our interests, shopping habits, personal needs, curious questions, or however else we are online. Whatever information we consume, the digital spaces include algorithms to be modes of personalized channels of authority. Consequently, our online habits aren't just about the information we consume. Our online activity can change our brain activity and management to the point where we become overwhelmed and oversaturated with content.

Compare your online activity to a one-on-one conversation with someone. Our brains are designed to receive approximately the amount of information of a dialogue with one person at a time. When surroundings do not allow this, our brains will naturally filter through information to decide if it is important to us or not. However, when online, our brains become overwhelmed because we are continuously encounter information our brains are wired to consume—shocking, hateful, or sexual content.

As we become aware of our digital habits and practices, we can become aware of what is truly important to us. For example, as disciples living in a digital age, Jesus wants our attention.

He wants to spend time with us. He wants to help us focus, instill us with purpose, and overcome modern-day distractions as followers of Jesus. Attention economics in digital spaces, as digital disciples of Jesus, is not as important as allowing our attention management to be shaped by Jesus. In our digital consumption, it is important—if not vital—to disconnect from digital spaces to reconnect with the divine. And even though the digital age is designed to constantly bait for our attention, the online trap to consume information leads to further digital clicks.

Social and entertaining information leads to further online clicks and links. It is like travelling down a rabbit hole with no end. Digital marketing 101 is to keep you engaged online; and based on your online habits and practices, digital platforms link your clicks to continue to engage and buy a product or service(s).

There is nothing wrong with what you click unless your digital habits and practices go unchecked.

Simply put, you become what you click.

Your online clicks communicate your likes and your dislikes, your tastes and preferences, your outlooks and values, your good and bad habits, and big tech companies arrange your online platforms to get you to continue to click.

What you click keeps you entertained in digital spaces.

I call this reality the digital trinity.

The digital trinity of endless connections, digital consumption, and enticing clicks wants your undivided attention. And based on the amount of limited time and space you have, your attention from the digital trinity is extremely important. In fact, the digital trinity is designed to overwhelm you with attention economics to continue you to engage in the online world.

According to a recent research study with the Barna Group, the average amount of time younger generations spend in secular digital spaces and places is 2,800 hours a year, compared to 153 hours of Christian-based online content.[6] That is roughly 5 percent of time given to engage in Christlike formation online with those under the age of thirty. If we are not aware of

---

6. Kinnaman and Mattlock, *Faith for Exiles*, 26.

the attention economics online, based on our digital habits and practices or how the digital trinity works, we become like the digital trinity.

We consume relationships. We demand efficiency. We want to be entertained. Even by God.

William Stahl puts it this way in his book *God and the Chip*: "It has become common to define our species as *Homo faber*, 'man the tool maker,' and to identify cultures with their technology—Neolithic, Stone Age, Space Age. . . . We increasingly come to identify who we are by and through the machines we use."[7] In other words, we put our faith within our own technological advances.

Anything and anyone (even those closest to us) become products to consume rather than relationships to connect. We isolate ourselves around the digital trinity rather than being transformed by the Holy Trinity.

And consequently, we experience increased levels of loneliness and mental health concerns.

Loneliness—even before COVID—was on the rise in our culture. In fact, the United Kingdom appointed, for the first time in modern history, a government official to be the Minister of Loneliness in 2018. In the UK alone, they have spent over a hundred million dollars to combat the epidemic of loneliness in their country.[8]

Symptoms of modern-day loneliness may include social anxiety, isolationism, poor self-awareness skills, and depression.

According to the psychology department at San Diego State University, mental health issues have increased 50 percent in younger generations, linking their mental health to their digital practices. Even seasoned generations, like my mom and dad's generation, are experiencing increasing feelings of isolation and loneliness as they retire.

A further study from the University of California has revealed high-level modern-day loneliness has the physical consequences of smoking fifteen cigarettes a day.[9]

7. Stahl, *God and the Chip*, 18.
8. Kristof, "We Know the Cure for Loneliness," para. 14.
9. Kroll, "Prolonged Social Isolation and Loneliness are Equivalent to Smoking 15

In addition to this, loneliness is known to shorten a person's lifespan by ten years and is linked to physical symptoms of hypertension, heart attacks, and further mental health issues affecting well-being and increasing symptoms of *infobesity*.

You might be asking, as I did, where does modern-day loneliness come from? If the digital trinity promises a life of continued connectedness, why is there an increased disconnect of loneliness in our world today?

Well, it stems from the secular world we live in.

Secularism is the idea where we have decided, as individuals and as a modern-day society, we don't need God anymore. So, we take God out of our lives, our work, and our key relationships. We take God out of our decision-making and ultimately our culture. God is merely a part of a religious experience or a fragment of our society, and as a result, we have put our hope in other things, like technology.

Interestingly enough, the rise of modern-day loneliness can be associated with the technology of the air conditioner.[10] Yes, the air conditioner.[11]

Before the invention of the air conditioner, people would congregate around front porches on neighborhood houses to enjoy the cool of the day. People would gather to discuss the day with family and friends. Yet, today, people do not need to congregate with family and friends on neighborhood porches. Modern-day society can experience the cool comfort of their air conditioner in their own homes. Due to this, people are isolated from each other.

Even in the context of metropolitan cities, people are isolated in skyscrapers and high-rise condos. People have forgotten how to do life with each other. In these modern-day concrete palaces, people who are close in proximity

---

Cigarettes A Day."

10. Alexander, "There's no quick fix for loneliness, but turning off the AC is a start."

11. The invention of air conditioners is a great example of technological advancements towards individualism and personalization. In Mississippi, before air conditioners, architects designed large porches for people to find comfort during hot and muggy days. As air conditioners were put in these homes, people did not mingle on decks (see Dyer, *From the Garden to the City*, 156).

CHAPTER TWO: THE DIGITAL TRINITY

with one another are miles apart from each other interpersonally. Hence, another reason for the rise of modern-day loneliness in city centers.[12]

A reactionary answer to the modern-day loneliness epidemic has been people adopting pets. Yes, cats and dogs!

According to *Forbes* magazine, 78 percent of people have adopted a pet during COVID. Due to the isolationism caused by COVID, many people adopted more than one pet for their home.[13] In addition to this, one in three people have admitted to having a difficult time making friends due to modern-day isolationism, which, of course, has increased the modern-day loneliness in our culture.

How ironic.

Well, there are further reasons for our modern-day epidemic of loneliness.

We see, then, technology did not only create the air conditioner but the invention of the television. For the first time, individuals would congregate around a screen. So, instead of going out to discuss world events or activities or build ongoing relationships with people, individuals would gather around a screen.

And now, technology has personalized televisions to a screen in your back pocket. This is where the digital trinity thrives in technology. Entertainment, digital consumption, and the lure of online clicks are accessible to us anytime, anywhere, any place.

But this leads us to the second reason for modern-day loneliness, it is because we live in a hyperindividualistic world. One of the unforeseen realities of living in a secular world is that we put our hope in things other than God.

In recent history—for example, the last one hundred years—we have put our hope in governments; and yet, governments have let us down. We have put our hope in multiple romantic relationships; yet still we struggle with modern-day loneliness. So, as a culture and as individuals, we decide to put our hope in ourselves. This, my friends, is the rise of individualism in our society. It is all about "me."

12. Trenqualye, "Alone in a Crowded City."
13. Tilford, "Survey."

So, as we live in our hyperindividualistic world, we filter our decision-making not through what makes you and me whole, as followers of Jesus, but what makes us happy.

We follow a career based on the pursuit of what makes us happy. We filter our relationships based on personal happiness. We consume relationships based on how others need to keep us happy (what crazy pressure that is on human relationships). We participate in religious services to experience a spiritual high, but when the church gets too close to us or the church does not make us happy, we leave to find another place to keep us happy.

Even our decisions around identity and purpose are based on our feelings of happiness rather than our well-being. And when someone or something does not make us happy, we simply let go with little consideration and cancel each other out. Even those closest to us we let go in the pursuit of the "next best thing" to make us happy.

Maybe my words are not making you happy. That is OK though. This book is about well-being rather than pursuing personal happiness.

The digital trinity knows how to work its magic when it comes to making you happy. The digital trinity is based on the entertainment of happiness with endless connections, ongoing online consumption, and engaging clicks. The digital trinity is extremely personalized and is designed to keep us happy.

As a pastor, I have seen this too often. People filter their decision-making through the digital trinity rather than the Holy Trinity. People decide on systems of me, my selfie, and I rather than the pages of Scripture. Incidentally, these same people who chase after the pursuit of happiness tend to come back to church. This time, they are not searching for happiness but for meaning, purpose, and significance. They have realized, in some cases, the hard lessons of decreased well-being as true happiness is linked to purpose and meaning and significance. The fleeting feelings of modern-day happiness in cheap forms of entertainment is unsustainable for human beings.

CHAPTER TWO: THE DIGITAL TRINITY

John Dyer, a theologian and web designer, suggests, "Today's technology [as seen as the digital trinity] places a high value on personalization, customization, and the preferences of the individual."[14]

Digital technologies have developed their platforms to be personalized to our preferences as a way to use happiness like a drug. The short-lived feeling of online happiness is linked to short spurts of dopamine.

Dopamine is the enzyme linked to feeling happy. It is a brain chemical connected to forms of pleasure and is the reward system for our bodies. Healthy amounts of dopamine are associated with physical activity, meaningful relationships, completing a task or duty, overcoming an obstacle, and even forms of prayer and Scripture reading. However, unhealthy forms of dopamine are short and constant. The streams of dopamine being released by digital forms of online connections, digital consumption, and clicks from the digital trinity are meant to be addictive in nature. Our online practices and habits enter our digital feeds and devices to keep us happy.

As an example, one of the co-designers of the largest social media platforms in the world today confessed their design of the "like," "ping," and "comments" on their social media sites were to create small doses of dopamine hits for their digital users.[15] Their design for online interactions with their digital platforms is to keep you and me happy. And yet, as a modern-day digital and technological society, we still wrestle with loneliness. We still deal with unhappiness. We still struggle with decreased levels of well-being. And instead of connecting in meaningful relationships with God and each other, our increased dependency on the digital trinity keeping us happy is increasing.

When measuring online habits and practices, digital users have increased digital consumption from 2.5 hours of being on social media platforms per day to an average of 4.3 hours and climbing.[16] This just speaks of our activity with social media. Not only does the digital trinity create dopamine hits through social media, but our digital devices, which make you and me productive, want to continually distract us too. Craig Detweiler, in his book

---

14. Dyer, *From the Garden to the City*, 178, italics mine.
15. Silverman, "Facebook's First President," para. 7.
16. Brandon, "New Survey," para. 3.

iGods: How Technology Shapes Our Spirituality and Social Lives, agrees: "We are inundated by too much information from our own making."[17]

As a result, the digital trinity has fueled the hyperindividualism of our modern world. We continue to create information (or online content) in the pursuit to be known, liked, followed, popular, and feel a sense of belonging. Yet, we still recognize the deep loneliness we are experiencing within our digital practices and habits. It is like we continue to pursue and create our own online content rather than pursue God to answer our deepest questions, frustrations, and problems in life. It is like we put our hope in technology instead of God.

Technology—with all the advancements and achievements in the last one hundred years—has caused a widening gap towards individualism and personalization rather than bringing us together. Albert Borgmann, in his book *Power Failure: Christianity in the Culture of Technology*, suggests technology "is meant to designate not just an ensemble of machines and procedures, but a type of culture, the kind that is characteristic of the advanced industrial societies and has been developing and gaining definition for two and a half centuries."[18]

It is like the digital trinity of technology is the religion of the day.[19]

As Campbell notes in her book *Networked Theology*, the "quest for efficiency through the application of human reasoning and logic ultimately dehumanizes individuals and communities by reducing them to impersonal, economic units."[20]

I would agree. Sadly, the digital trinity views digital users as impersonal and economic units rather than human beings needing to experience spiritual, relational, mental, and physical well-being. We are intentionally or unintentionally and fundamentally manipulated by online content, misinformation, and fake information towards attention economics rather than Truth.[21]

17. Detweiler, *iGods*, 15.
18. Borgmann, *Power Failure*, 7.
19. Dyer, *From the Garden to the City*, 145.
20. Campbell and Garner, *Networked Theology*, 32.
21. This is in the whole science of digital business based on destructive economies. In short, it is when a new digital technology creates a business that destroys another

As followers of Jesus, God answers the deepest of questions and challenges our world faces today. There are aspects of life the digital trinity tries to answers but cannot.

Of course, digital spaces and places have merits for well-being and modern-day productivity, but do not merit all things human.

Only Jesus can answer the most fundamental and important questions of life and what makes you and me human.

Google tries to provide answers on the meaning of life and significance, but cannot truly answer. Purpose, respect, honor, love, Truth, and freedom lives in God, not in our own happiness pursuits or creative content or the latest online information or shiny digital devices by the digital trinity.

Only Jesus can answer the deepest questions of our modern-day technological world.

How can we find Jesus in a digital world?

Personal Reflections

- How has the digital trinity enticed you to get your attention? Share an example with someone.
- What symptoms of *infobesity* do you experience from the digital trinity? I encourage you to write them down. This will help you to be aware of your digital practices and habits online.
- How can we experience the Holy Trinity in a world bombarded by the digital trinity? Share a practical example or idea at www.infobesity.ca.

---

business, either in an offline or online platform. An example of this would be Blockbuster and Netflix.

CHAPTER THREE: The Digital Garden

>"Not all information is created equal."
>—Len Sweet

>"In the future, our attention will be sold."
>—Mark Manson

The first people on planet earth experienced *infobesity*.

It all started at the beginning of the human race. Adam and Eve had the perfect relationship with God, with each other, and with themselves.

Now, let us reflect on this reality for a moment. Imagine with me what a perfect relationship would look like.

Imagine a perfect relationship where there would be no conflict or pain or heartbreak. With no misunderstanding or blame. With no miscommunication issues.

It would be heaven on earth!

Imagine being whole, and not broken, as a person.

Imagine how productive you and me would be. Imagine the beauty of being in a perfect relationship with yourself where mental health issues were nonexistent, death and decay were absent, and you we were confident in your existence as a person.

Imagine!

CHAPTER THREE: THE DIGITAL GARDEN

Adam and Eve had it all!

There was no sin, no pain, and no shame. There was no conflict or brokenness or fear and anxiety. There was no death or destruction.

There was no loneliness.

In fact, Adam and Eve didn't know what human brokenness was before sin entered the story. They never experienced sin. They never experienced separation from God or others or from themselves.

They were living in perfect harmony.

And yet, they decided to choose to eat from a tree in the middle of the garden called the tree of knowledge of good and evil. It was at this tree, when they participated in eating its fruit, where they experienced *infobesity* at the highest of levels.

The serpent, which the Bible literally describes as "crafty" or "deceitful" (Gen 3:1a),[22] was grabbing for Adam and Eve's attention economy. He used shock and awe to distract them from God with the question, "Did God really say (that)?" (Gen 3:1b, brackets mine).

Eve responded—and rightly so—to the serpent, "But God said, 'You must not eat fruit from the tree that is in the middle of the garden, and must not touch it, or you will die'" (Gen 3:3).

But let's pause here. Did God really say that? Well, let's go back to what God did say about the tree to Adam (even before he created Eve for Adam).

In Genesis 2:9 and 2:15–17, God describes the tree as "the tree of life" and "the tree of the knowledge of good and evil."

In these short verses, we can see what went wrong. Instead of focusing on the tree of life (found in God), Adam and Eve focused on the tree of knowledge of good and evil (found in sin).

---

22. "Crafty, adjective (craftier, craftiest), 1. cunning or deceitful, 2. informal relating to the making of objects by hand.
 —DERIVATIVES: **craftily** adverb **craftiness** noun
 —ORIGIN: Old English *cræftig* 'strong, powerful'"
(*Concise Oxford English Dictionary*, 11th ed., s.v. "crafty").

And, as we have been exploring throughout the pages of this book, information is the starting point of knowledge. Yet not all information is created equal.

With the example of Adam and Eve, they put their full attention on misinformation. They listened to the cunningness of the serpent rather than trusting in the Truth of God.

I wonder, are we the same. Is it possible we experience information overload because we listen to the cunningness of modern-day attention economics in digital spaces rather than trusting in the Truth of God?

I think it is possible. In fact, I call this reality the digital garden. The digital garden is when you and I experience modern-day distractions like Adam and Eve were distracted in ancient times.

Of course, I think we all have experienced the modern-day digital distractions of information. The flashy screens, the entertainment reels, and the endless content distract us from trusting the divine activity of God. Like every lesson in Scripture, the ancient story of Adam and Eve becomes an example of how to deal with modern-day forms of *infobesity*.

Adam and Eve's distractions from God made them curious about knowledge. This is not a faulty pursuit. But their source of information was. They listened to a false source of information. They traded their attention from God to the devil. They put their trust on the serpent of lies rather than their Savior. And ultimately, Adam and Eve put their confidence in the lies of misinformation rather than the relational revelation they had with God in the garden.

The Bible explains, as Adam and Eve participated in eating the fruit from the tree of knowledge of good and evil, "at that very moment, their eyes were opened . . ." (Gen 3:7a NLT). Eugene Peterson comments, "Immediately the two saw what was going on . . ."[23]

They ate the fruit. Their eyes were opened. They experienced sin, human brokenness, and evil. At that very moment, Adam and Eve didn't know the serpent's intent was evil until he enticed them with eating the fruit (which was prying for their attention).

---

23. Gen 3:7a in Peterson, *Message*.

CHAPTER THREE: THE DIGITAL GARDEN

Let's take a step back for a moment. Is it possible the modern-day digital trinity of cheap entertainment, unlimited efficiency of online information, and enticing digital economies entice us to act like Adam of Eve in a digital garden? Is it true we don't understand what is truly going on until "our eyes are opened"?

This is an important reminder.

The story of Adam and Eve encourages us to be aware of our digital practices and habits living in a digital garden. Unchecked, the information of digital spaces shapes us more than the Truth found in Jesus. Rather than enjoying the presence of the LORD in harmony with God, with ourselves, and each other, we are continually bombarded by the digital garden distracting us with information wanting to harm us, hurts us, distract us, manipulate us, and isolate us.

For Adam and Eve, they were manipulated by information. They were confused by what they just experienced. The knowledge they experienced by eating the fruit of information immediately separated them from God's presence.

For the first time in human history, they experienced loneliness, brokenness, and they ultimately encountered the highest forms of *infobesity*, separation from God.

This is the utmost confrontation with information overload.

Adam and Eve decided to put themselves at the center of their story. Rather than submitting to God's story for their lives, the writer of Genesis shows us, "they suddenly felt shame and hid themselves . . ." (Gen 3:7b NLT).

Not only did Adam and Eve experience separation from God, but they experienced separation from each other. Deep feelings of shame, hurt, and guilt rose within them for the first time in their history.

They blamed each other for their overwhelming information overload. And, in reaction to the information overload they were experiencing from each other, they hid themselves not only from God (even though it is impossible to hide ourselves from God) but from each other in isolation.

And, finally, their information overload led them to face personal information overload as well—death. Not only physical death but spiritual death. A death separating them from God. The most painful death. A death that could not be redeemed by human achievements or pursuits but through a righteous, just, and loving God found in Jesus.

Adam and Eve sold their attention to the serpent, and we have been dealing with the effects of *infobesity* ever since.

In our modern-day technological world, we experience the same effects from information overload. We experience shame, guilt, and loneliness from God. We sin against each other and ourselves, causing further damage from *infobesity*, isolating ourselves from God and each other.

Symptomatically, as digital consumption increases in culture, modern-day loneliness increases as well. Digital users engage in digital spaces to stay connected but feel oddly further disconnected from others. We interact with online information and yet still feel confused and frustrated by information.

In psychological terms, an example of *infobesity* is termed dopamine loops.[24] It is when digital users continuously interact with digital spaces to deal with symptoms of information overload with seemingly low relief.

After a speaking engagement on *infobesity*, a young adult wanted to talk to me about my session. In my presentation, I encouraged individuals and families to have dinner together as an opportunity to combat modern-day loneliness. She explained to me how lonely she was when she was with her family over dinner. She recognized, as her family gathered physically together over a meal, they were on their digital devices. Rather than having face-to-face interactions with one another over a meal, they were consuming online interactions instead. In her own words, she lamented, "I want to know how to engage with my mom and my dad at the dinner table who are inches away from me physically but miles apart from me relationally. I want to know how to stop this."

Curiously speaking, can you relate with her?

---

24. Haidt et al., "Social Media and Mental Health," 254.

CHAPTER THREE: THE DIGITAL GARDEN

Have you ever felt disconnected from meaningful relationships which are just feet away from you but are emotionally miles apart?

The term for this is called phubbing. Phubbing is when someone is more interested in their relationship with their digital device than with the physical relationships around them.

At times, I have unintentionally done this. I have phubbed key relationships. I have been distracted by my digital device with those who are significant around me. At other times, those significant to me have phubbed me. It is so easy to phub each other, even during a romantic meal at a restaurant.

There are times people have run into me at the mall simply because they are preoccupied with their screens rather than their surroundings.

We miss the divine when we are distracted by modern-day digital screens. Phubbing is an example of being too distracted from key relationships around us.

Phubbing is real.

Relational *infobesity* is real. Relational *infobesity* causes loneliness and mild mental health issues, and if left unexamined, heavy use of digital practices can potentially paralyze you and me from our God-designed purpose.

Think of our NHL friend Connor McDavid. He is considered one of the best hockey players in the world, and he struggled with modern-day *infobesity*.

Or consider mayor Merlin Blackewell. He was digital distracted by social media. He had to limit his social media presence from online trolls and bullying because he was not at his best for his city.[25]

Or consider the one in three adolescent women and one in five adolescent men who struggle with online social media comparison. A review from a collection of counsellors addressing online addiction by Twenge and Hyatt have concluded moderate to heavy usage of social media content have caused body dysphoria, social comparison, and physical insecurities in digital users. This has included comparison to digital models, body image, and comparison rather than being confident in their own well-being.[26]

---

25. See "BC Mayor Goes Facebook-Free."
26. Haidt et al., "Social Media and Mental Health," 32.

Due to this, digital users have experienced deep insecurities. Digital consumption has paralyzed younger generations, causing them to question their divine purpose in this world simply because of the symptoms of *infobesity* they are encountering.

If we are honest with ourselves, we have all experienced symptoms of social comparison before. Online, however, the effects of *infobesity*—of purposelessness—increases with consumption of digital spaces.

It is important to ask ourselves, has information overload caused us not to be at our very best? Has your digital device phubbed you from giving your best at school or at work or with the key relationships in your life?

I know it's happened to me.

I know it's happened to my kids.

I know most of the 6.4 billion people who have a smartphone have experienced mild forms of *infobesity*.

As information is not regulated or moderated by any ethics commissions or government policies to protect digital users,[27] we need to protect ourselves.

Consequently, people who have experienced harmful or hurtful information online have been left confused by digital spaces and places. Like my grandma or Connor McDavid, or like you and me, they are being blitzed by *infobesity*. And unfortunately, the signs of *infobesity* are all around us, inside digital spaces and outside of digital places.

In extreme examples, *infobesity* is particularly experienced on social media platforms. It is like modern-day serpents are chasing for our attention to entice us with whatever they can offer.

There are times when I am passively scrolling through my social media feeds and a post or comment, or meme or reel wants to entice me. I have noticed the amount of time I have wasted because I get caught up on social media reels. For me, this includes gym posts, funny church memes (I send too many of them to my family and friends), and at times, the latest news or world events. It is so easy to get sucked into digital spaces.

---

27. Horwitz, "Facebook Says Its Rules Apply to All."

CHAPTER THREE: THE DIGITAL GARDEN

When I get sucked into digital spaces, I notice, not only have I phubbed people in my life, it is like I am phubbing myself from my purpose.

Has you ever experienced phubbing yourself before? As an example, it is like you are passively scrolling through your social media feeds, and something entices you, and without knowing it, two hours have passed by just like that.

After an *infobesity* session with parents, a father with two teenage students came up to me to talk about his online practices. As he noticed from our time together, he found himself passively scrolling through new reels hours a day. He went to online news apps, as they helped him decompress from his busy day at work. He recognized how much time he was spending online.

In his own words, he admitted, "I have wasted too much time on what I thought was important online. I could have used that time to finish the basement suite in my house. Or, I could have spent more time with my kids. But instead, I get caught up with the news reels of the day." In laughing it off together, he ended his thoughts: "I need to put a time limit of how much news I am scrolling through online."

We all have interests, items, and idols we look for online. Just like the tricks from the beginning of time with the serpent, online information uses whatever will shock us, distract us, awe us, and lure us to engage.

We can spend countless hours on information not building us up but deterring us from what is important or meaningful or purposeful in this world.

One way younger generations have tried to find meaning online is to create social media burner accounts. In fact, eight out of ten young people have acknowledged having at least one fake social media account. Social media burner accounts are meant to express themselves in presumably safe places. This might offer some elementary relief, but experiencing face-to-face loving relationships is of the utmost importance. It is in relationships we need to have to combat modern-day loneliness and the isolationism *infobesity* causes.

This includes the dinner table.

Now, to put this in perspective and as we have mentioned, it is more likely your social media followers, friends, and accounts have bots entertaining you rather than having meaningful relationships with you. With all the fake information around you and me, the digital bots, and faceless social media accounts, how can we respond as followers of Jesus to engage in face-to-face relationships instead?

How can we respond to the unregulated and unmoderated digital age where big tech companies and governments politicalize rather than finding, accepting, and experiencing loving relationships we desire to have?

In connection to *infobesity*, psychologists and organizations alike, including the World Health Organization, have deemed *infobesity* as a modern-day disorder.

In our *infobesity* research process, we discovered higher levels of digital consumption are uniquely connected to relational dynamics in the home. For example, higher levels of digital activity in children are apparent when parents are not home (due to work or school). The level of mild to moderate symptoms of *infobesity* increased when meaningful relationships were not present.

Furthermore, higher levels of unfiltered and unexamined information consumption increased when digital devices were not moderated or regulated by parents. Younger digital users have no experience with digital boundaries and/or delayed gratification skills. Due to this, the well-being of younger digital users decreases, and over time, affects their social and cognitive skills in the home.

The World Health Organization agrees with this. Their experts call the effects of *infobesity* ESS—electronic screen syndrome.[28] Bottom line, one of the unforeseen consequences of the modern digital age mixed and matched with the sedentary lifestyle of the latest pandemic is digital screen time. The effects of *infobesity* being discovered are links to negative well-being, mental health concerns, physical health concerns, lack of personal resiliency, and relational isolationism.[29] Especially in the home.

This is where the effects of *infobesity* in a digital garden thrive. As followers of Jesus, how can we respond to ESS? How do we create digital

---

28. DeFrank, *Digital Detox*, 31.
29. WHO, "Excessive Screen Use," 2.

habits and practices where we are not enticed by modern-day serpents and digital gardens?

Where do we go from here?

Personal Reflections

- Have you ever experienced modern-day loneliness? Share a story.
- How has the digital trinity enticed you to consume higher levels of digital content?
- Have you been distracted from being at your very best because of *infobesity*? Why or why not?

CHAPTER FOUR: The Ancient Selfie

"Those who do not learn from history are doomed to repeat it."
—George Santayana

"To constantly consume information about whatever fits our fancy is often just another form of entertainment."
—Chris Martin

In 2005, for the first time in modern-day human history, someone has physically died from *infobesity*.

His name was Lee Sueng Seop. He was only twenty-eight years old.

Lee subsequently died as he was playing an online interactive video game for fifty-eight hours straight! He didn't eat. He didn't sleep. He didn't take a break. He did not take time to stay hydrated. He didn't stop!

The only reason he got up from his seat was to go to the washroom. For two and a half days, this young man was being entertained online with a modern-day video game.

I didn't know this was even possible.

The front desk clerk realized Lee was slumped over his computer and went to assess the situation. As the front desk clerk went to check on Lee, he noticed Lee was not responsive and phoned the local paramedics. Tragically, a few hours later, Lee passed away. The subsequent investigation into the cause of his death was heart failure caused by exhaustion and dehydration.[1]

Terrible, right?! The number of people dying from information overload from digital technologies is increasing every year.[2]

How can online activity, unchecked, have such consequences that modern, unmoderated, unregulated digital information can become so dangerous?

Is entertainment—literally—killing us?

It is unfortunately true.

This led me to an ancient story. A story that still rings true today. A story of how we all are, at some points of our lives, distracted with entertainment, even to a point of distracting us from our God-given purpose. It is a story where God is put on the sidelines. His people are pursuing entertainment rather than a divine relationship.

It is an ancient story we can learn from for our modern-day times. If we can learn from this story, we can become aware of the design of modern-day entertainment found in *infobesity*, and how to redesign our digital habits as disciples living in a digital world. It is a story which will guide you and me in a world wrestling with *infobesity*.

In Exodus 32, we see the same consequences at work with Lee who experienced the extreme effects of information overload. And instead of telling you the story, I'd rather show it to you. This painting is an ancient selfie, if I can call it that, of a painter displaying to his audience what is happening in Exodus 32.

It was painted by Nicolas Poussin in 1633. Back then, most of society did not read or write. Due to this, famous Scriptures would be explained through art—paintings or sculptures. These works of art were designed for people to experience and interact with in relationship. I want to do the same with you today. Take a look:

---

1. Meurisse, *Master Your Emotions*, 15.
2. Nguyen, "Fifteen People," paras. 2–3.

Nicolas Poussin, *Adoration of the Golden Calf*, 1633[3]

Now, before you scan over this painting and keep reading, take a moment to examine the ancient art of Poussin as a modern-day selfie.

What jumps out to you about this painting? Do you see God in this painting?

You see, before Jesus, God made himself present to his people through a pillar of smoke during the day and a pillar of fire by night. The Bible puts it this way: "By day the LORD went ahead of them in a pillar of cloud to guide them on their way and by night in a pillar of fire to give them light" (Exod 13:31).

This meant God was guiding, protecting, providing, and leading his people during these days by his presence. In the same way, God leads us through his presence because Jesus now lives in us (1 Cor 6:19–20). He guides, protects, provides, and leads us in a world bombarded by modern-day digital information.

---

3. Public domain. https://www.nationalgallery.org.uk/paintings/nicolas-poussin-the-adoration-of-the-golden-calf.

In this painting, do you notice how God is not at the center of the scene? If you take a hard look, we could make the distinction that God is perhaps in the distance. He is seen in the clouds in the background.

According to Poussin, it seems like God is deliberately in the distance of human activity.

Furthermore, do you see how Moses, the leader of God's people, is placed in the shadows? You can see him in the darkness (top left-hand corner) descending from the mountain. He doesn't seem too pleasant. In fact, what he experiences descending Mount Sinai breaks his heart.

You can observe he is only holding one of the tablets from God, which, as Scripture puts it, is written with the very "finger of God" (Exod 31:18; cf. 8:19).[4] This would mean the ancient tablets were divine in nature. The authority of God written on the tablets for the people of God was to experience life like Adam and Eve in the garden. In his anger and frustration with the scene, Moses throws one of the tablets on the ground. The tablet breaks and shatters on the ground. In essence, these tablets represented a new covenant, a new relationship, a new identity with God and his people miraculously being delivered out of slavery in Egypt. And yet, the people of God truly never experienced this reality because of their rebellion from God. Their renewed relationship with God was broken until Jesus enters the story of humanity.

Or consider what Poussin's painting reveals about the people of God.

Do you see the human activity around the golden calf? They are dancing, celebrating, spectating, inviting each other to participate, and, simply put, being entertained. It is shocking to see the people of God not worshiping the active, living God—who just delivered them from Egypt days before and is active and present with them—but deliberately deciding to worship a lifeless, shiny, larger-than-life golden calf instead.[5]

---

4. The same activity God did in the land of Egypt is referenced to what God did to the tablets on Mount Sinai. It is important to note how God's work was to re-establish God's people's identity and reliance on YHWH; and yet, God's people are compared to Pharaoh's hard heart with the worship of the golden calf.

5. Approximately forty-seven days from the shores of the Red Sea to Mount Sinai (see Exod 17:1a; Rudd, "Exodus Route").

For such an episode, we must ask ourselves, "What does this golden calf represent?" And, equally as important, "What golden calfs do we create in our modern-day technological world?"

In Exodus 32:4, we see Aaron "made [gold] into an idol cast in the shape of a calf..."

Some historians believe the golden calf represented the Canaanite gods around them. Canaan was the area where the people of God were surrounded by Mount Sinai. And because of Moses' delay on the mountain (Exod 32:1), the people of God began to search for other expressions of worship in their impatience with Moses.

Others suggest the golden calf represents Israel's own expression to worship God in their own ways. Rather than trusting in God through patient endurance, they worshiped God in their own ways. They created a cheap golden calf with their own fingertips rather than submitting to the divine fingertips of God.

Exodus records the people of God took their gold jewelry, taken from their Egyptian masters, and melted it to form a golden idol. It is important to note the Egyptians used their wealth to encourage the Israelites to leave Egypt. They buckled under God's activity and were now using their found wealth for their own selfish needs. Aaron, the leader of God's people when Moses was up on the mountain, who is seen in this painting as the gentleman in a white robe and long stylish beard, is the one who formed the golden calf. It was Aaron who designed the wooden idol plated in gold, created by his own fingerprints, to be worshiped rather than the tablets created by God's fingerprints.

In addition to this, theologians believe the golden calf represented the gods of Egypt. As the people of God experienced four hundred years of Egyptian slavery, their identity as slaves gripped them rather than resting as freed children of God. And therefore, they worshiped what they knew. They worshiped their past, as slaves, rather than experiencing their new found freedom as children in God.

The Ten Commandments were meant to teach the people of God how to experience freedom. The ancient tables in Exodus 32 were not designed to be a set of rules or regulations but a new way of life for the people of

CHAPTER FOUR: THE ANCIENT SELFIE

God. The tablets were meant to free them from the four hundred years of Egyptian oppression.

In any case, the golden calf could represent all three forms of worship.

Truth be told, the golden calf episode in Exodus 32 continued to be a part of Israel's history up to the resurrection of Jesus. We see in the days of Isaiah, seven hundred years after the deliverance from slavery in Egypt, the people of God did "as Egypt did . . ." and worshiped other gods (Isa 10:24; 11:16; see Isa 54:15a–b).

The people created idols made in their own image, not in God's image. They used their creative skills to create other gods rather than be creative for God. I am increasingly convinced every generation wrestles with the concept of worship. Struggling with worshiping God, and wanting to worship what is created by human hands. The forms of idols, even religious idols, are realities we all face. Rather than worshiping the One who created us to be, we create idols to worship.

In fact, we see signs of religious idols even during the days of Jesus on earth. Some people believed Jesus was going to be a military leader to overthrow the Roman world. Others thought Jesus was a political leader. They expected Jesus to start a new political history for Israel. His closest friends even believed this. But Jesus never caved into the pressure. He had a bigger kingdom to reveal.

In these cases, it is important to realize we are no different from Ancient Israel. We can relate to the first-century followers of Jesus. If left unmoderated, we can create modern-day golden calfs too. Maybe not out of stone or medal but out of plastic and high-speed connections. Maybe not around idol worship but the worship of ourselves in digital spaces.

Perhaps the golden calf episode of old communicates more about who we are as human beings more than what the golden calf actually represents.

In Exodus 32:1, we see God's people didn't just become impatient with Moses—they were impatient with God. Due to their delay on the mountain, the people of God put their own selfish motivations to work. Instead of trusting God, they trusted in themselves. Instead of walking in the ways God created, they created their own images from Egypt. Instead of walking with purpose, they rebelled for counterfeit entertainment. Instead of waiting on God, they took matters in their own hands.

Is it possible for you and me to do the same?

Have you ever thought about what this painting reveals about us? Perhaps Poussin is inviting you and I to experience the same episode in Exodus 32. We need to ask ourselves, who is the one snapping this ancient selfie? Well, it would be you and me. Poussin is purposefully, and masterfully, painting a picture about us.

Is it possible we exchange a purposeful relationship with the living God to be entertained by things we create with our own hands? As you and I live in a modern-day selfie culture, it is easy to create modern-day idols of self rather than follow the God of the Universe, isn't it?

Is it possible we create shiny trinkets, like the golden calf of old, with our modern-day digital devices rather than follow the One who created all things?

I would suggest we do.

CHAPTER FOUR: THE ANCIENT SELFIE

Just like the people of God in Exodus 32, we see the DNA of the golden calf debacle throughout human history.

Even King Solomon—who was considered the wisest man alive; and yet, did not live out his own wisdom—worshiped a golden calf. Due to this, his kingdom was consequently divided, and it sparked the beginning of the end of Israel's dominance in the ancient world (1 Kgs 11:1–8).

The Israelite kingdom was another attempt by God to give Israel the opportunity to reveal the greatness of God through an earthly kingdom. But it failed.

Repeatedly, the worship of golden trinkets didn't end with King Solomon. King Jeroboam took it even further. He created two golden calfs to be worshiped. He created separate temples to worship separate gods. He created space to worship the God of the universe but built his own personalized gods to worship too (1 Kgs 12:28–29).

He forsook God by doing his own thing. He wanted to worship God, but he also wanted to worship his own selfish ways. So, he designed multiple forms of worship to please his own desires and pursuit of happiness.

We do the same thing, don't we? We create our own digital spaces to be worshiped, to be praised, to be highlighted; and yet, still try to worship the One who created us. How ironic.

Instead of becoming an icon pointing people to the Creator online, we become shiny, personalized, modern-day golden idols by choice.

Sometime later, we see King Jehu allowing idol worship in the nation of Israel. He repeatedly ignored the ongoing warnings of God's prophets for their well-being. Spiritual apostasy increased and the well-being of the nation decreased (2 Kgs 10:28–31).

We see the debacle of Exodus 32 with the golden calf episode's lingering effects in Israel's painful history of rebellion, complacency with God, and pursuing cultures' cheap forms of entertainment.

Upon reflection, what does this painting reveal about us? Is it possible Nicolas Poussin is trying to get our attention with this painting, too?

In our modern-day and selfie world, we want to create our own image rather than live in the image of God (see Gen 1:27). In a world where we create our own branding, we brand ourselves to be digital entertainers rather than live with purpose, with Jesus, for Jesus (see John 10:10).

Is it possible for us to be like the people of God in this ancient selfie?

If we are honest with ourselves, this story is really about worship. And in our modern-day digital and technological world, it is easy to worship entertainment by the latest shiny and showy idol rather than God.

The ancient lesson in Exodus 32 is a reminder to check our hearts with what we worship. We become what we worship. If unchecked, modern-day *infobesity* can be a form of worship leading to serious consequences as followers of Jesus.

One way to check ourselves in this modern digital world is to be aware of what has our attention. In the story of Exodus, the distractions of everyday life still resonate today.

As we see in the opening verses of Exodus 32, Moses goes to the mountain to hear from God. Moses is God's representative. He is commissioned to start a new covenant for God's people. And instead of waiting for Moses to come down from the mountain, they shift their focus for a moment. A moment focused on impatience and entertainment. Perhaps this is not too far off from the human condition in a digital world too. We demand efficiency, unlimited consumption of information, and access to be entertained in a moment. We worship the digital trinity of social media reels designed to keep our attention.[6] Algorithms determine what we engage in online (based on our digital habits and practices)[7] rather than God. Big tech companies design misinformation to keep us distracted and shocked rather than centered and peaceful.[8]

Now, entertainment is not negative or shameful unless it distracts us from what matters most—experiencing God on the mountain.

---

6. Hibbs, *Hidden Power of Electronic Culture*, 160.
7. Plato, *Phaedrus and the Seventh and Eighth Letters*, 96.
8. Campbell and Garner, *Networked Theology*, 32.

CHAPTER FOUR: THE ANCIENT SELFIE

In Exodus 32, the mountain represented where God resided. The mountain represented the activity of God. The mountain represented the power and authority of YHWH with a pillar of smoke by day and fire at night (Exod 19:18). The mountain represented what God did for the people of God in Egypt forty-seven days earlier. The mountain represented God.

We need to be aware of the mountain—God's presence too—in our lives. It is where God is active and living in us, not the modern-day technology around us. It is the mountain working miracles, signs, and wonders through his presence and not the blinking screens of high-pressure glass and plastic. It is the mountain that brings purpose in our lives, not the online information from the digital age.

So how do we do this? How do we focus on the mountain in the bombardment of moments?

To be aware of the mountain is to seek out the mountain. To focus on the mountain is to be aware of the distractions of modern-day moments found in technology. If we go back to the fingerprints of God, which were the tablets of old, are now found in the Word of God. If we allow God's Word be the ultimate authority in our lives, we will experience God's presence like Moses offering purpose, peace, and relationship with God.

The question is, do we go to the tablets of Scripture or to the modern-day tablets of digital connections?

A practical example to be in God's presence, like Moses was at the mountain, is to practice a digital sabbath. To take a twenty-four-hour period of time to shut the screens down and turn off the phone. To be silent. To let God speak in his whispers through a sea of modern-day distractions.

Another way to focus on the mountain is to enjoy creation. Let God speak through intentional time in creation. Allow God to reveal himself through the beauty of nature around you and I. In the quietness of Sabbath and creation, the Holy Spirit has permission to speak to us. It is in these times where we are reminded of his truth in a land of online lies. It is in his presence which heals us; to realign us; to restore us as we live in a digital world (John 16:13–15). To allow the mountain to be in our lives is to focus on creating digital habits which redeems digital practices. This moves us from pursuing moments to the mountain.

According to psychologist and counselor Jonathan Haidt, digital consumption should be limited to two hours per day. Of course, this excludes work and education, but in the context of the digital trinity of entertainment, the experts agree two hours per day or lower is the limit.[9] Otherwise, mental health issues, social isolationism, and overall well-being decrease with each hour of digital consumption.

With the practice of digital sabbaths and reconnecting with the Creator through creation, we develop the awareness of the selfie culture around us. The personal brandings we create, if unchecked as followers of Jesus, become modern-day golden calfs. We become the shiny objects. Our content becomes the golden calf.

We build stories of entertainment, to engage our social media platforms, to sell ourselves to the selfie culture around us rather than reveal the One who created us.

As we see in the ancient selfie of Exodus 32, if our digital practices and habits remain unchecked, the digital world will consume us. We will forget what the mountain is. We will forget his presence and what he has done for our lives. We will forfeit our own well-being.

We will be distracted by modern-day digital trinkets. We will believe in our own reels rather than being real with God. We will build our own digital brands in the hope of being famous or influential rather than build a Jesus brand. Unfiltered, we will use digital platforms to make ourselves look better than we truly are. Unrestrained, we will become the author of our own stories rather than live for his glory. We need to ask ourselves, "What is more important to us—our selfies or our Savior?"

May I suggest, as followers of Jesus, we can develop a Jesus brand rather than build our own brands. What would it look like if we were able to build online brands to make Jesus famous rather than ourselves living in a selfie world?

As we will see in section three of this book, redeeming digital spaces is allowing a Jesus brand to affect our emotions, our minds, our strength, our relationships, and our own souls. The Jesus brand moves us from the tablets of old and from the modern-day glass and plastic tablets to the tablets written on our human hearts (2 Cor 3:3).

---

9. Haidt et al., "Social Media and Mental Health," 224, answer 2.

It is to understand how digital information has affected our emotions, our minds, our physical bodies, our relationships, and souls, and to allow Jesus to redeem us.

As McLuhan prophetically wrote in his famous book, *Understanding Media: The Extensions of Man*, we need to be aware of the golden calfs we create because, ultimately, we become what we create.[10] If unchecked, we too can allow the values of the digital trinity to become the idol of our hearts rather than Jesus as tekton.[11]

When we filter our decision-making through the lenses of the digital trinity, we can treat our careers, friends, family, our spouses; and even God, as objects for our personal entertainment, consumption, and happiness rather than experience the purposes God has designed us for.

Ultimately, the Jesus brand is what will bring hope to the world, not the modern-day calf of technicism.[12]

But how do we move from the hope of technicism to Jesus as tekton?

Personal Reflections

- What observations do you see in Poussin's painting about God and yourself?
- What does the ancient story of Exodus 32 reveal about your modern-day digital practices as a disciple of Jesus?
- When you engage with your digital practices, what is your focus? Do you focus on the mountain or the digital moments and personalized memes of self?

---

10. See McLuhan, *Understanding Media*.

11. Jesus as a carpenter comes from the Greek word *tekton*, which means builder, masonry worker, and creator. We will discuss this in chapter 7.

12. Technicism has been considered the religion of the secular. It is the belief system where technology—applied science—is the answer for humanity's problems.

CHAPTER FIVE: Symptoms of Infobesity

"Our brains are busier than ever before. We're assaulted with facts, pseudo facts, jibber-jabber, and rumor, all posing as information."
—Daniel Levitin

"The truth will set you free."
—Jesus

The tablets of old had ten statements to abide by. It was God's way to redesign the people of God from the values of Egypt as slaves to a new identity as children of God.

It was God's way to form a new nation. For Israel to be set free from the idols of the world to find fulfillment and purpose in God.

And yet, because of the Exodus 32 debacle of rebellion and secularism,[1] the people of God needed to detail their everyday living to 613 commandments found in Levitical law.[2] These laws were created for the people of God because they could not keep to the Ten Commandments. In ancient times, these commandments were not meant to be rigid rules but an

---

1. Simply put, secularism is the philosophy of not needing God in our lives. Consequently, if God is not a part of our lives, then we substitute ourselves to other forms of worship. For the people of God in Exodus, it was the Golden Calf. For us today, it is the rise of individualism in technology—putting our hope and worship, ultimately, in ourselves.

2. Later rabbinic tradition gave the total number of commandments as 613, 248 of which were positive commands and 365 prohibitions (Garland, *Mark*, 476).

invitation to experience a dynamic relationship with God rather than the fleeting entertainment of human hands.

And yet, these commandments of old were a letdown. No one could humanly abide to 613 commands day in and day out. This is why Jesus came. Jesus came to fulfill the commandments of old for humanity to truly experience God in real relationships.

We see this reality explained in Mark 12:30–31.

As Jesus was interacting with people around him, he was approached by a religious leader who curiously asked, "Out of all the commandments, which one is the most important?" (Mark 12:28).

Another way to look at it, when Jesus was asked this question, the man was seeking an answer for "What is most important about life on earth?" and "How can I discover my ultimate purpose in this world?"

These are questions we all ask.

The answers to these questions are fundamental to what brings hope, purpose, meaning, and significance in our lives on this earth.

Ironically enough, we tend to ask these questions in digital platforms too. But rather than hearing truth from Scripture, we are bombarded by *infobesity*. Rather than going to the divine to answer these questions, we think modern-day information will answer our deepest questions.

Due to this, we get feedback and opinions and responses which may lead us to pseudo aspects of purpose; however, the way digital platforms are designed, they lead to further symptoms of *infobesity*. Symptoms of confusion and fogginess rather than clarity towards personal purpose and significance.

At least the religious guy went to the right person. He went to Jesus to ask his deepest questions! How about you and me?

Do we tend to go to digital spaces before we go to the divine? Obviously, the easiest way to get the answers to our questions is from digital spaces. The instantaneous. The access. The plethora of information at our fingertips that is available to us constantly. We can ask any question our heart desires, and at the same time, get any type of informational response for everything.

But as we have discovered through the pages of this book, not all information is equal. The same goes for our questions.

There are questions about life. There are questions about relationships. We have personal questions about our own stories. These are questions digital spaces are limited in answering.

Only the divine can answer.

When Jesus responded to the religious leader on his questions about purpose and meaning, he quoted Deuteronomy 6:4–6. This passage of Scripture is known as the last words of Moses. His words were meant to inspire the people of God, as they were about to enter the promised land.[3] These words, which are considered the most important words of Moses in the Pentateuch, are known as the SHEMA.

To the ancient people of God, the SHEMA was known as the central purpose for people on earth. For example, the Israelite nation would recite the SHEMA three times a day—morning, noon, and night—as part of their daily worship of God.[4]

What is interesting, however, is that as Jesus is quoting the SHEMA, he is ultimately revealing himself as the new SHEMA.

He responds to the religious leader not with commandments but with relationship. He puts it this way:

"Love the Lord with all your heart and with all your soul and with all your mind and with all your strength. The second is this: Love your neighbor as yourself. There is no commandment greater than these" (Mark 12:30–31).

Jesus becomes the SHEMA. He becomes the central purpose for life.

Ten Commandments to two.

Ten statements to a divine relationship with God.

In a similar way, Jesus does this same with us.

---

3. We all experience a spiritual promised land in Jesus. This includes personal purpose, significance, and meaning on earth to make a difference for God.

4. Elwell, *Baker Encyclopedia of the Bible*, 2:1945 (s.v. "Shema, the").

CHAPTER FIVE: SYMPTOMS OF INFOBESITY

He moves us from stone tablets to the tablets of our hearts. He desires to write on the tablets of our hearts with his own fingertips rather than our fingertips being attentive on screened tablets.

Jesus ultimately changed the game on purpose, meaning, and significance!

The SHEMA of old represented a foundational truth for God's people. The words of Moses were a commission to be set apart. The SHEMA was God's way to reveal himself to the world through his people. The ancient people of God were meant to have a dynamic relationship with God and to make a difference in the world.

They fell short.

In saying that, the amazing reality is that Jesus adds to the SHEMA. As he quotes Moses' words, He adds to the SHEMA, linking Leviticus 19:18 to love your neighbor as yourself as seen in Mark 12:30–31.

Jesus is therefore inviting the religious leader to a new way of life. He is inviting him to a purposeful life in relationship with him, wholeness from sin, and divine well-being.

He is inviting the religious leader to a better way of life.

At the end of the conversation, the religious leader accepts Jesus' invitation (Mark 12:32–34).

Jesus does the same for you and me.

He invites us to find answers to our deepest questions through him.

He invites us to divine purpose.

He invites you and me to experience wholeness in a world of *infobesity*.

Could we respond to his invitations?

In a modern world where answers are cheap and instantaneous, only Jesus can answer the deepest questions of our hearts. Yet, *infobesity* can live in the deepest parts of our lives as well.

As Jesus defines well-being with all our heart, soul, mind, strength, and our relationships, we are invited by Jesus to live in well-being with him.

When we allow the divine into our well-being rather than digital spaces and places, we experience deep purpose and significance.

Our Hearts

When Jesus was referring to the heart, he was not referring to a physical organ. He was addressing our emotional well-being.[5]

We don't have to go too far to recognize the negative impacts of our emotions with our digital usage. Moderate to heavy levels of digital consumption increases negative feelings. These feelings include spurts of depression, social and personal anxiety, feelings of self-harm, and even confusion in personal purpose.

Too much digital information can create an infobese heart.

In a controlled experiment at the University of Pennsylvania, researchers initiated an in-house study on the symptoms of *infobesity*. They wanted to determine if digital practices with their students affected their emotional well-being.

A group of undergraduate students were asked to track their digital practices and habits. The study was simple. Take a screenshot based on their digital consumption from the day and document their emotional well-being in a journal. After four weeks of ongoing research, the students shared their observations. In review, the research team and the students acknowledged an increase of emotional well-being when digital practices were intentionally regulated.

---

5. Elwell, *Baker Encyclopedia of the Bible*, 1:939 (s.v. "heart").

In fact, after the four-week experiment, certain participants deleted their social media platforms all together. They recognized the increased benefits of not being on social media. Furthermore, other participants continued to regulate their digital practices to maintain their positive emotional well-being.

Other universities and colleges followed suit. Throughout the States, for example, educational institutions have limited or banned certain social media platforms from their campuses.[6] Even elementary and high school districts throughout North America are prohibiting digital devices in the classroom for the well-being of their students.[7]

The results from the University of Pennsylvania were fascinating. At the time, the research on digital consumption and personal well-being was limited. For the research team to determine social media practices were a source of negative emotion were revelational. The decreased levels of digital consumption were directly linked to the increased emotional well-being of their students. As a result, student productivity increased, social well-being in relationships improved, personal coping skills were developed, and course grades in the classrooms surged.

Even now, the results of the in-house study are so overwhelmingly positive for the researchers and the participants that the university recommends a limit of ten to thirty-minute consumption of social media per day for their students.[8]

Have you noticed your digital habits and practices decrease your emotional well-being?

Think about it for a second. With the fake information scheming for our emotions, the speed of anxiety and fear are on full throttle, the hateful and harmful reels are not about real life. These techniques engage our emotions and negatively impact our well-being.

It is a constant bombardment, isn't it?

---

6. Castillo, "These Colleges Just Banned TikTok."
7. Buck, "Hold the Phone."
8. Berger, "Social Media Use."

Oddly enough, this type of digital trickery is nothing new. The information we consume online is tied to our human condition. Even throughout the stories of Scripture, the Bible defines harmful, hateful, and fake information as deception.

It is a string of digital trickery.

Like the ageless story of Genesis, the cunningness and craftiness of the serpent still distracts humanity from God-given purpose.

Jesus addresses deception too (Matt 13:22). He says deception is like weeds in our hearts. The emotions of fears and worries of this world grow in our hearts and can eventually take over our lives. In a digital world, these *infobesity* symptoms of the heart gradually choke out God's truth in our lives.

A few years ago, I had an opportunity to talk about *infobesity* to a group of students at a secular high school. It was an interactive conversation with forty tenth grade students about their personal daily digital practices and habits (yes, it was organized chaos at its finest).

At the end of the session, I had a few students stay behind to talk to me. For one of the students, you could visibly see the struggles she was facing about her digital activity.

As she was sharing with me about her online practices, she kindly explained to me how her social media platforms were an opportunity for her to be popular. She showed me her posts, her millions of views, the hundreds of comments and likes she was receiving. She had thousands of followers. As a fourteen-year-old student, she was quite impressed by it.

As she continued to speak to me, she was becoming aware that her digital content was not aligning with her personal values. As she mentioned she was a follower of Jesus (or trying to be a follower of Jesus), she hadn't allowed Jesus into her digital spaces.

She continued to share with me how her online follower count flatlined. The comments on her social media platforms became silent. Her engagements with the digital world decreased.

Unapologetically, she produced content which went against her relationship with Jesus. She desperately wanted to reengage her online popularity. She posted content to be popular, not to be like Jesus. And her digital practices and habits were obviously affecting her emotional well-being negatively.

The term for this is called dissonance. Dissonance is a fancy word where our actions, belief systems, and words don't line up with reality. For the short-term, dissonance can be managed. It seems to me, in the digital world, dissonance tends to be promoted and elevated. Even in our own research with *infobesity* with thousands of participants from various backgrounds—including non-faith, religious, students, parents, pastors, and the general public—digital practices and habits create dissonance.

This young fourteen-year-old woman continued (like a confession), "If I get less than four hundred likes on any of my posts, I delete it."

For this fourteen-year-old student, she was processing her own personal dissonance with me. The decisions she was making online was based on her digital popularity rather than her personal values. Due to this, her own emotional well-being was being affected. Jesus simply didn't live in her digital spaces.

Let me pause here for a second.

This young woman was filtering her online content based on the likes and comments from strangers more than her personal value system. Why?

Well, according to a collaborative research review on social media and emotions from New York University, the ongoing scientific studies confirm her online filtering processing system is based on dopamine—what makes her feel good. Her digital practices are being filtered through the likes and comments she is posting. This feedback loop, connected to her emotional tank, can become digitally addicting.[9]

She was addicted to online fame and didn't even know it.

You might not think digital practices can become addictive. But when digital spaces are interacted with in high forms of digital content, these messages are linked to the reward pattern in the brain. Psychologist David Levitin puts it this way: "The social network addiction loop, whether it is Facebook, Twitter, Vine, Instagram, Snapchat, Tumblr, Pinterest, email, texting, or whatever new thing will be adopted in the coming years, sends

9. Haidt et al., "Social Media and Mental Health," 195.

chemicals through the brain's pleasure center that are genuinely, physiologically addicting."[10]

The added online likes and posts online increases the surge of dopamine being released in the brain. This creates ongoing consumption of social information and develops addictive behavior. Even if it goes against our personal values as followers of Jesus, high levels of digital consumption can cause negative emotional well-being.

For example, every hour of digital consumption per day is connected to 1 percentage point of negative feelings of depression and anxiety to rise.

Think of the digital habit of passive scrolling. Passive scrolling is the digital practice of scrolling through digital content on a screen. Passive scrolling is meant to consume further digital content and usually accessed through a social media platform.[11]

At a parent seminar on *infobesity*, a dad asked me a question about his digital practices. He said, confidently, "I am not on social media. I only use my phone to scroll through the news at night." He continued, "I don't think I am addicted to online platforms but can my news activity increase symptoms of *infobesity* with me?"

In response, I asked if he was scrolling news reels for over two hours a day. The room chuckled and waited for his reply. In agreement, he said yes. I responded, "Then sir, you are experiencing at least mild forms of *infobesity*."

Typically speaking, moderate to heavy usage of passive scrolling is linked to harmful effects on emotional well-being too. So much so that feelings of self-harm rise in younger users and addictive behavior in adults,[12] even if the content is just news reels.

For instance, think of the fake information clouding political elections. The polarization of opinions, thoughts, and political platforms have confused the general public. The content online, and whether it is real or

---

10. Levitin, *Organized Mind*, loc. 4054, Kindle.

11. *Collins Dictionary*, s.v. "scrolling," https://www.collinsdictionary.com/dictionary/english/scrolling.

12. Haidt et al., "Social Media and Mental Health," 94.

false, with political candidates, parties, and even the nation has confused people rather than bring clarity as a nation.

Seasons of elections should bring the nation together, not drive people apart. Feelings of anger, bigotry, and judgement want to rise.

It should be mentioned, however, negative emotions of depression, self-harm, and anxiety do not increase with low digital usage. Depending on the social media platform, according to various of studies in the United Kingdom, the United States, and in partnership with the University of Oxford with over two-hundred thousand participants from countries across the world, digital counselors and experts alike recommend ten minutes to two hours of digital consumption for the well-being of digital users.[13]

Social media can be positive.

Platforms can leverage connections with family and friends (like my grandma).

Digital spaces can be used for helpful and practical information, not just hurtful or harmful information.

In saying all this, it is so important to be aware of our digital practices.

If we are not aware of our digital consumption and positive or negative effects on our emotional well-being uniquely tied to our digital practices, whether we realize it or not, our digital habits do shape us emotionally.

But not only does *infobesity* affect our hearts, but unchecked amounts of digital information can damage our souls too.

---

13. Przybylski and Weinstein, "Large-Scale Test."

PART ONE: JESUS AND INFOBESITY

Our Souls

When Jesus is talking about the soul, he is addressing the very core of who we are. Unlike any other species on earth, God created us with a soul. Humans—beyond any other being on earth—can distinguish what is good or evil, have the ability to make choices between what is right and wrong, and have the conscious ability to rationally reflect about the past, the present, and shape our future.

Not only has God created you and me with a soul to make decisions and be cognitively aware, He also created us for relationships.

The soul is divinely created by God. Our soul is designed to have a relationship with God; and this results in purpose, relational clarity, personal identity, and significance in this world.

To God, our souls are the primary identity of *who* we are.

In a digital world, identity has become clouded.

Modern-day identity has been based on personal feelings and emotions rather than the One who created us. As we discovered in chapter 3, when our identity is based on our personal happiness and feelings, the rise of modern-day loneliness increases. Our purpose can become foggy. Our decision-making can be stunted.

These are signs of an infobese soul.

As we see through the words of Jesus, the main cause of loneliness is not the absence of events or relationships but an absence of purpose. Jesus puts it this way two thousand years ago: "I have come that they may have life, and

CHAPTER FIVE: SYMPTOMS OF INFOBESITY

have it to the full" (John 10:10). Jesus is revealing our identity—purpose, meaning, and significance—is linked to our soul.

Jesus promises you and me abundant life. A purposeful life with meaning and significance. Jesus guarantees a life of clarity rather than the cloudiness of a confused and lonely digital world.

Not only is Jesus speaking about the purpose and meaning of life in John 10:10, but he is also talking about the concept of personal confidence. As we are divinely designed, anything outside of confidently submitting our identity and purpose in God will leave us lacking. Anything outside of having a relationship with Jesus will lead us to further confusion and frustration of personal purpose and meaning in this world.

Have you ever experienced a lack of meaning and purpose in your life? Has your purpose ever been clouded by the nagging voices around you or inside you?

I sure have.

This is what was happening to the people of God in Exodus 32 too. They exchanged their newfound purpose in God for their old patterns of worship. Instead of trusting in God, they put their trust in their own ways.

It is like the modern-day digital world nags at you and me to find purpose and meaning in digital spaces rather than trusting the divine words of Jesus.

So often, I have done the same.

Amazingly enough, according to a five-million-person study on healthy adolescenthood, identity formation towards personal meaning and significance is directly associated with building a successful and productive life as adults.[14]

These associations include core positive peer voices, mentorship from trusted adult relationships, such as coach, or teacher, or parent, positive hands-on training, and spiritual experiences.[15] None of which is based on moderate or heavy usage of the digital trinity.

---

14. See https://www.searchinstitute.org.
15. See "Developmental Assests Framework."

Due to this, adolescents have a positive outlook on society and evidently make better choices in life. They have higher grades. They want to contribute constructively to society. Their overall well-being increases.

It is like God designed us to be confident, productive, and fruitful when our souls find purpose in him.

However, the opposite is also true.

Those who have a negative identity formation; especially with higher consumption of digital content, have a negative outlook on society. People make poor choices in life and relationships. Consequently, adolescents with decreased self-confidence have lower grades.

Identity formation, at all levels, is extremely important to combat *infobesity* of the soul.

Out of the five aspects of well-being, Jesus makes it clear our souls are the most important.

The well-being of our souls is at the center of our identity. For Jesus, our soul is the very center of our purpose and what brings meaning to be alive on this earth.

Our souls are the only aspect of our lives that is eternal.

Plato, the Greek philosopher in the fourth century, wrestled what it meant to experience purpose. In fact, he spent a lifetime searching for the meaning of life, what gives humans purpose and personal significance. In his own words, he defined the soul as the eternal element of humanity—whereas the body perishes at death, the soul is indestructible.[16]

You see, the very center of our purpose is our souls. As Plato has described it and as Jesus has addressed it, at the very core you and I have a spiritual identity. With the words of Jesus recorded in John 10:10, only Jesus can satisfy the deepest desires of our souls.

We can continue to search for and seek meaning and purpose in digital spaces, or we can truly be alive with the divine.

---

16. Elwell, *Baker Encyclopedia of the Bible*, 2:1987 (s.v. "soul").

It is really a matter of personal choice. In fact, we are the sum of our choices, aren't we?

Now, even though Jesus speaks to our souls and Plato concludes we are spiritual, not just physical, we have a social identity too.

Our social identity represents our family backgrounds. It includes our ethnicity and our upbringing. It can involve our last names; representing our values systems, family traditions, how we see the world, and ourselves in the world.

Our social identity is extremely important. Not only does Jesus shape our souls but our human relationships do as well. As followers of Jesus, we are spiritual and social beings. But only do we have a spiritual identity or a social identity, we also have a sexual identity.

Sexual identity is a powerful concept. Sex has the potential to bring life into the world. Sex is how we engage in marriage and relationships. As followers of Jesus, sex is designed by God and to be celebrated. Sexual identity, as we see throughout the pages of Scripture, is linked to how we have been created male and female. Sexuality is connected to our biological upbringing.

According to Jesus, however, our social and sexual identity is not at that core of what defines us. Our souls do.

In the view of eternity, our spiritual identity is the most important aspect of our lives.

Think of Jesus' identity on earth. He was a single thirty-year-old Jewish man in first-century Israel.

This would have been extremely strange for the Jewish tradition. According to his social and sexual identity as a Jewish man, He should have been married. Jesus should have had kids. As a professional carpenter, he would have taken over the family business. But he didn't.

How odd. How abnormal! How could a healthy thirty-year-old biological male be single?

If Jesus based his identity on his social and sexual identity, he would have been strangely seen as an outcast from Jewish society.

But not only was Jesus particularly strange or odd for being single, his earlier outlooks as Jesus from Nazareth would have been deemed as confusing as well.

Nazareth was a humble town. A town outside the main roads of civilization. History reveals Nazareth was the place where outcasts hid, religious folks fled to in political rebellion, and was known for its isolated location.[17] Even Scripture records, "Can anything good come from Nazareth?" (John 1:46) when responding to Jesus' upbringing. Jesus, the Messiah, from a lowly position like Nazareth, really?

Even during Jesus' earthly ministry, numerous groups of people had expectations of Jesus being a military leader or a political leader or a religious leader. People followed him because of his miracles, signs and wonders, and teachings.

So many people were following Jesus for their own reasons. Yet, Jesus never caved into the popularity or pressures of the crowds. He didn't make decisions based on becoming famous. Just like modern-day digital spaces, Jesus would have not been influenced by the likes, the followers, or the affirming comments. He would not put his identity in digital spaces. He trusted the divine purpose of God.

In Matthew 3:17, right before Jesus' public ministry would start, where he is led by the Holy Spirit to confront sin, human brokenness, and the power of death in the wilderness, Jesus' core identity is revealed.

As John the Baptist baptizes Jesus in water, Scripture records a voice from heaven declaring, "This is my Son, whom I love, with him I am well pleased" (Matt 3:17 NIV).

The voice represents all of heaven. From the divine throne room of God. The Father himself proclaiming, "This is my son," meaning, "I am his dad. I am with him and for him. He has a heavenly home with me."

The Father continues, "Whom I love, with him I am well pleased." To this point of Jesus' ministry, he didn't accomplish anything. We know very little of the silent years of Jesus (other than his birth and youth years). For the

---

17. Strange, "Nazareth (Place)," 4:1050.

CHAPTER FIVE: SYMPTOMS OF INFOBESITY

voice of heaven to say these words about Jesus has eternal impact in the context of identity formation.

The Father is saying to Jesus, identity is not based on social status or sexual preference but based on a spiritual identity with God.

This is the same with you and me. Jesus is saying, "You are my son," "You are my daughter," "You are loved, with whom I am well pleased."

With these words, our souls are designed to find identity in the divine. The whispers of love, identity, meaning, and purpose are revealed by the divine. Digital spaces cannot reach the depths of the need you and me have for a spiritual identity.

Our souls are created to be with the One who created us. The One who spoke the Cosmos into being speaks to our very core of being loved, accepted, and cherished. The Creator of the Cosmos wants to reside in his creation.

It is a beautiful picture of a soul aligned with the Savior.

The rise of modern-day loneliness, the lack of purpose, and increased amounts of self-destructive thoughts continue, especially in younger generations, when we put our identity in the digital rather than the divine.[18] Stories of purposelessness and a foggy identity are uniquely linked to unregulated digital practices.

At some point, I think we have all experienced symptoms of an infobese soul.

It is because our souls are designed for the divine. As Jesus divinely quoted the SHEMA in Mark 12:30–31, our souls are meant to be enjoyed by God. As we foster a divine relationship with God, we rekindle purpose and identity in God, not in cheap forms of entertained with empty promises of purpose and identity in digital spaces.

If you are still reading this and you have not surrendered your soul to the One who created your soul, I would encourage you to invite Jesus into the very center of your life. You will not regret it.

---

18. Rideout et al., *Coping with COVID-19*, 8, 29, 33–34.

He will instill you with purpose. He will whisper to you of *how* he sees you. He will address the modern-day loneliness you are facing. He will be with you, now and forever.

You are divinely loved by God!

The best decision I ever made was when I invited Jesus into my soul. It was like everything changed. Everything within me and around me transformed as I experienced his love, clarity of purpose, and meaning in this life. I experienced a newness I never experienced before.

It is like his love captured my soul. I did not deserve his unending and undeserved love, and yet, God breathed life into me.

Scriptures echoes this experience. An early church leader named Paul confidently puts it this way: "If you are in Christ, the new creation has come: The old has gone, the new is here" (2 Cor 5:17).

What a great promise!

In a world wrestling with purpose, meaning, identity, and modern-day loneliness, Jesus promises a better way of life. He gives us a deeper identity. A new start. A new life in him.

No more spiritual death. No more confusion. No more lack of identity. No more loneliness.

He makes our souls new.

He gives us an opportunity to be set free from the information overload world we live in. He gives us a new spiritual identity. The best identity you and I will ever experience—forever!

As Jesus continues to quote the SHEMA, he mentions a third aspect of our well-being—our minds.

CHAPTER FIVE: SYMPTOMS OF INFOBESITY

Our Minds

In the last few years, the signs of *infobesity* in our minds have been extensively researched.

Neurosciences have discovered remarkable advancements of *infobesity* affecting our cognitive reasoning. As we have discovered in the pages above, our brains are filtering systems shifting through thousands of forms of information from primary, secondary, and irrelevant streams of information based on personal importance. In digital spaces, our brains are actively sifting through countless pieces of information, which may cause cognitive overload. The amount of information we are presented with online overwhelms our brains.[19]

Due to this, you and I can experience decreased levels of mental retention, cognitive distractions, delayed decision-making processes, mental and/or relational distractions, decreased problem-solving skills, and increased levels of personal stress and frustration.

In a genius move, tech companies—who have developed various algorithms and artificial intelligences to filter online information based on our digital practices and habits—are experimenting with how to filter digital information through brain waves.[20] This is the concept of digital developers to help you and me, through our brain waves, to filter through countless bits of information. It is an amazing concept, really. However, information is filtered through our brain biases rather than truth.

Since COVID, another reaction to symptoms of *infobesity* on cognitive reasoning has been a rise of online meditation techniques and regulation

---

19. Moran, "Future-Proof Your Brain"; Dishman, "Meet the Woman."
20. See https://naralogics.com.

activities.[21] This includes meditation apps, digital device moderations techniques, and internet self-regulation tools.

Ironically, these responses are limited. We must become self-aware enough to understand how our brains are designed. We need to understand how we are being shaped by digital practices rather than to simply develop rules and regulations around digital practices.

As followers of Jesus, we are encouraged to model the well-being of our minds on the divine, not the digital. Not through brain waves or online meditation techniques, which are genuine and useful, but through the active and living power of Scripture.

Scripture is more than words on a page. Scripture is more than letters on a screen. The Scriptures give us the invitation to encounter the divine. The Scriptures have the power to transform our daily lives. Scripture implores us not to be conformed by the patterns of modern-day digital trinity and technological world, but to be renewed by the renewing of our minds (Rom 12:1–2).

Scripture encourages us to take every thought captive. Scripture helps you and me to make our minds obedient to Christ (1 Cor 10:5). For example, according to psychologist Norman Wright, the average person has forty-five thousand thoughts a day.[22] Two-thirds of those thoughts are either unproductive or negative in nature.

It is like we are bent to focus on the negative. To be fearful. To focus on being broken. Yet, with the roughly thirty-thousands thoughts we have which are negative or counterproductive, God calls us to renew our minds through the active and living words of Scripture.

You might be asking yourself, "How do I renew my mind in a world of *infobesity*?" or think, "How do I make my thoughts obedient to Christ?" These are good questions to ask. We will be discussing the subject of how to live in the Truth of Scripture in our post-truth culture in-depth.[23]

21. Dishman, "Meet the Woman," para. 6.
22. Wright, *Better Way to Think*, 46.
23. What I mean as "Truth" is experiencing the power of Scripture through the lenses of Jesus, who, with John (1:1, 4)—Jesus himself saying, "I am the Truth" (John 14:6)—reveals Jesus as the source of all Truth. We will discuss the different aspects of Truth as a Person and the power of personal transformation and renewal through Scripture in chapter 8.

As we have discovered, not only does *infobesity* affect our emotions, our identity, and our cognitive reasoning, but it also affects our physical well-being.

Our Bodies

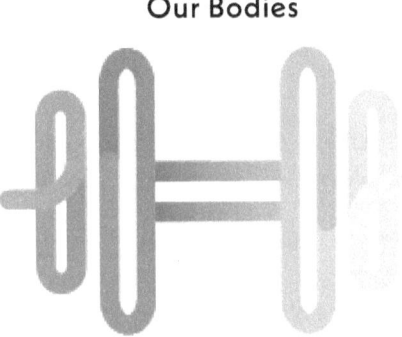

For a season of my life, I was a personal trainer at a local gym. I loved working with people. It was an honor to empower people to meet their fitness and personal well-being goals.

Personal well-being is connected to physical activity. Self-confidence, personal resiliency, and healthy levels of dopamine (which are maintained and stable) are experienced when we are active. For instance, for every one hour of physical activity we complete, three hours of lifespan is added. Amazing reality, to be honest. Our well-being is uniquely connected to our physical activities.

By design, we are meant to be active. In the digital age, the new health hazard of our day is sitting too much.

In fact, prolonged sitting is more damaging than smoking cigarettes.

Think about it. We sit all the time. We sit at desks for work. We sit while we eat. When we travel, we sit in cars, trains, and planes. As a society, we are sitting more than any other time in human history. We live sedentary lives. Due to this, physical inactivity increases.

According to an article by the Harvard T. H. Chan School of Public Health, life expectancy has decreased in the last two decades.[24] This might come as a shock, but inactivity is a part of this problem.

The symptoms of physical inactivity caused by digital *infobesity* do not just include sedentary living but physical comparison. Higher use of online activity has caused an increase in eating disorders, body image bullying, and physical shaming.

In addition to this, extreme levels of digital usage have caused Tourette's-like symptoms in preadolescents.[25]

If I am honest with myself, I have experienced physical symptoms of *infobesity*. In my line of work, I need to be constantly online. I study and read online. I communicate online. I am connecting with dozens of people through emails, texts, or apps. I am constantly connected.

As I have become increasingly aware of my digital activities with my work, I have noticed the influences of *infobesity* in my physical life.

One of the signs I have noticed with my digital practices is blue screen fatigue. Blue screen fatigue is the condition of eye strain, minor headaches, dry eyes, and even mild sleeping disorders due to moderate to heavy screen use.

As I would write and communicate for work, the symptoms of blue screen fatigue progressively became an issue for me. My right eye would become fatigued and dry. I began to experience minor headaches. At times, my right eye would twitch. Consequently, my eye strain effected my creative work as I could not focus.

In response, I bought myself a pair of blue-screen glasses. It was a game-changer for me. My eyes wouldn't strained to digital screens. My headaches disappeared. My work became focused.

Another response, which has helped me deal with my physical symptoms of *infobesity*, is the 2-2-2 principle.

---

24. "What's Behind 'Shocking' US Life Expectancy Decline."
25. See Frey et al., "TikTok Tourette's"; "Why Tic-Like Behaviors Are on the Rise."

CHAPTER FIVE: SYMPTOMS OF INFOBESITY

The 2-2-2 principle is a digital discipline of taking digital breaks in two-hour blocks. For me, this includes a two-hour break from screens when I wake up, a two-hour break from screens before bed, and a two-hour max for social media per day. In addition to this, I break up my day into two-hour blocks, so my work is focused and productive.

As soon as I implemented the 2-2-2 principle in my life, I recognized how much I needed to put boundaries around my digital practices. The emails, the instant text messages, and the notifications were constant; and yet, when I realized how distracted I was with my digital devices, I was able to become more productive as a follower of Jesus.[26]

In a post-COVID world, the sedentary lifestyle of the pandemic has lowered satisfaction in life. There has been an upsurge in psychosomatic complaints in recent years.[27] In simple terms, we are living in a modern-day inactive society. As we are physical beings, studies recommend young people to be physically active for one hour per day. For adults, physical activity should be thirty minutes per day (or equal to eight thousand to ten thousand steps).

The physical well-being of children, youth, and adults who are active for thirty minutes to one hour per day is enormous. Confidence, posture, mental well-being, and energy levels increase with physical activity. In particular, a simple stroll in nature stimulates trillions of neurons in our brains, stabilizing serotonin levels, activating our kinetic chain, and releasing creative thought.

Consider Barack Obama. He reflected his best decision-making and creative skills were stimulated when playing late-night basketball with his friends.

Winston Churchill, when he was the prime minister of war-torn Britain in World War II, made his most important decisions around a standing desk.

The genius plan of the Lease-Lend Agreement in 1941 originated when Roosevelt was fishing.

The invention of the iPhone was developed on Steve Jobs's daily walks.

---

26. We will be discussing the 2-2-2 principle in-depth through section three of this book on how to redeem our digital spaces.
27. Khan et al., "Screen Time."

Creativity, innovation, and overall physical well-being in a digital world is linked to how to combat modern-day symptoms of i*nfobesity*.

As you and I become aware of the physical symptoms of *infobesity*, we can respond redemptively by being active.[28]

How can you experience physical well-being in a digital world?

As we have explored how *infobesity* affects our emotions, our identity, our minds, and our physical well-being, Jesus speaks of one last area of our lives. He uniquely links our overall well-being and the effects of *infobesity* with the relationships around us.

Our Relationships

We are social creatures. We are designed for quality, in-depth, and thriving relationships. We are meant to connect, communicate, and belong in the orbit of social relationships.

Yet, the dangers of relational *infobesity* is to view our relationships through the influence of the digital trinity.

You see, when we are unaware of the messaging in digital spaces, we become shaped by those digital spaces. As we have explored, we become what we consume. In digital spaces, the digital trinity of online entertainment, consumption, and instantaneous information effect our relationships.

In fact, the digital trinity can take over our relationships. We see relationships as a means to an end, to entertain us (to keep us happy), to be consumed (for my needs), and to be instantaneous (at all costs). But this is not

---

28. See chapter 10.

how God designed relationships. Social interactions, friendships, and family circles are not to be led by the overpromising and the under-delivering messaging of the digital trinity but fulfilling by the divinity of Jesus.

As someone who works with people every day, I have stories upon stories of people canceling each other out. Couples deleting each other and torpedoing their marriages. Families blown up because Mom or Dad say, "They are not happy with each other anymore," and therefore block each other out.

I have heard it all. I have witnessed spouses say, "My values have changed." I have experienced couples hurt each other, causing pain and hurt not only to each other, but those closest to them, their families or friends. It can make for a great debate as relational *infobesity* is one of the main causes of the modern-day loneliness epidemic in our society.

In one of our *infobesity* case studies, a young adult participant recognized his high level of social anxiety towards women was linked to his digital practices.

For him, he was confident, bold, and witty with his online interactions, but to meet for a face-to-face conversation caused increased feelings of personal fear, perceived assumptions of social rejection, and, in an extreme situation, caused him to vomit before a casual face-to-face coffee date.

He identified, over a series of redemptive *infobesity* practices, his level of digital information was harming his ability to form meaningful relationships. In response, he decided to develop social media boundaries, went to a counselor for help on how to handle digital addiction, and his overall well-being began to increase. Ironically enough, the woman he was supposed to have a casual coffee date with, where he vomited due to his social anxiety, is now his wife.

God did not create relationships to be consumed. Jesus did not call us to be relationally entertained for personal consumption. God created relationships to empower each other. As followers of Jesus, social relationships are an opportunity to become more like Jesus because of our relationships.

Relational *infobesity* has caused more than enough hurt and pain in the relationships around us. The rise of social isolationism, modern-day loneliness, relational brokenness, and polarized tribes are hurting, not helping, our advancement as a society.

As the ongoing research on *infobesity* is exposed in our culture, it is important to allow Jesus to shape our relational well-being. In chapter 9, we will be going through redemptive practical steps of how to develop relationships as God has designed relationships to be. Then, we can overcome relational *infobesity* experienced in our digital world and redeem digital spaces as followers of Jesus.

Jesus, as the modern-day SHEMA, who presents you and me with a better way to live in a digital world, provides a pathway of personal and relational well-being.

Are you willing to follow a better way?

Personal Reflections

- In the five quadrants of personal well-being described by Jesus, how has *infobesity* affected your heart (emotions), soul (identity), mind (cognitive reasoning), strength (physical well-being), and relationships (relational well-being)? Write this down in a journal or share a story at www.infobesity.ca.
- Practically speaking, based on the words of Jesus in Mark 12:30–31, how can you be aware of your digital practices to experience personal well-being with Jesus?
- How will you address *infobesity* in your life?

PART TWO: Responding to Infobesity as Followers of Jesus

CHAPTER SIX: **Well-Being in an Infobesity World**

"I am online twenty-five hours a day!"
—A Self-Aware Young Adult

"By spending countless hours scrolling, we engage online less than being human."
—Chris Martin

Recently, in a university lecture room full of undergraduate students, I curiously asked them, "What is the average time young adults, like you today, are on digital platforms per day?"

A young lady shot up her hand and said, "Two and a half hours a day."

I said, "Higher."

A gentleman in the middle of the room put up his hand and responded, "Five hours per day."

I said, "You are getting closer."

Then, out of nowhere, someone in the back of the room spontaneously shouted, "Twenty-five hours a day!"

The room erupted with laughter. A few people in the room shouted back in praise. Others clapped. A handful of guys cheered. Several others shook their heads in modest disgust.

But that young gentleman was onto something. He revealed something important to those in the room that night. He was saying we are online all the time. It does not matter what we are doing online or where we are or when we are online, we are always online, twenty-five hours a day.

In our research on *infobesity*, we found signs of information overload in each of our participants. From young professionals to pastors to young adults; from non-believers to adolescents to parents, the level of information overload is increasing around us.

Excluding education and work purposes, the average amount of digital use in the early 2000s was 2.3 hours per day. In the mid 2010s, the average was 4.3 hours per day. In a post-COVID world, the online average is 7.3 hours per day.[1] It isn't twenty-five hours per day, as our brilliant undergraduate indicated, but the evidence is convincing. Digital consumption is on the rise.

We interviewed hundreds of young adults, parents, students, and grandparents from various backgrounds and spectrums. We had everyone from non-faith individuals to religious churchgoers, multiple demographics participating in the research. The goal was to understand the latest digital practices and habits living in a digital world.

In one interview, a prominent young adult minister expressed, quite strongly, the effects of *infobesity* in his life and ministry were evident, but "young adults do not care how much time they spend online." He continued, "Young adults are online all the time. Their digital device is like the air they breathe."[2]

In addition to the study, when asking faith-based young adults if their faith was an important factor to their digital practices and habits, 93 percent responded with "very little" or "no." Jesus did not live in their digital spaces.

In acknowledgment of this, we developed a second cycle of research by asking the same young adults reasons why they didn't share their faith online. They responded, "Sharing Jesus online is just too political for me." Others

---

1. Auxier and Anderson, "Social Media Use in 2021," para. 17; Brandon, "We're Spending Seven Hours Per Day," para. 1.

2. Gabruch, "Infobesity," 97.

CHAPTER SIX: WELL-BEING IN AN INFOBESITY WORLD

communicated, "Jesus lives in my heart but not in my digital practices." A few young adults indicated they encountered online bullying and hateful information towards them when they shared their faith online. One of the participants disclosed, "It was not worth it to share my faith online because of the online hate I get. I have experienced mental health issues when I share my faith on my social media platforms."[3]

Self-awareness, as followers of Jesus living in a digital world, is extremely important. Being aware of our digital practices and habits help us understand how the digital world is shaping us, for our personal well-being or not.

When we understand our digital practices, then we can respond in healthy ways—revealing Jesus to those around us—as we regulate and moderate our digital habits.

Initially, when participants went through the *infobesity* research, we recognized a trend between digital practices and faith habits. We concluded followers of Jesus were either outright rejecting digital spaces or receiving digital spaces with inadequate discernment processes. It is difficult to determine the level of *infobesity* you and I are experiencing unless we are self-aware to intentionally understand our digital habits and practices.

First, based on the digital users results with our research on *infobesity*, there were participants outright rejecting digital spaces. These users would frequently reject social media sites and online gaming platforms. The number one reason we received digital users wanting to reject digital spaces was to focus on their personal well-being.

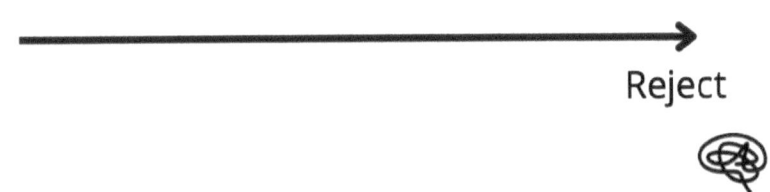

Reject

In one conversation, a mother of two teenagers responded to an *infobesity* presentation with the personal motto, "I will never be on social media because of what it has done to my immediate family." She described how

---

3. Gabruch, "Infobesity," 18.

social media tore her family apart. For her, the harm digital practices caused to those closest to her was just too much. They would fight with each other on their social media platforms. She didn't even want to elaborate on the online hurts with us, but the deep pain caused by her family members was real. We could visibly see the frustration emanating from her as a mother of two teenage sons.

In another presentation, a young adult woman told us she didn't want to engage in social media platforms because of the toxicity social media platforms had on her friends. She personally rejected social media practices because of the negative effects the platforms had on her friends. She didn't want to get involved in the online world.

When presenting a lecture on *infobesity* at a prestigious Bible college, a graduate student responded to one of my presentations as irrelevant. He didn't need to know about digital spaces or places because his experience on social media is "incubators for sin." He isn't wrong.

How about you?

Have you rejected digital spaces for your own well-being? Throughout the country, there is a rise of digital users rejecting social media platforms, especially in younger generations. Their well-being is too important to them. They would rather stay away from digital practices than engage in the toxic behaviors found on these platforms.

According to the chart below, the well-being of digital users are dependent on the digital platform, consumption of digital spaces, and their personal well-being at the time. Take a look:

CHAPTER SIX: WELL-BEING IN AN INFOBESITY WORLD

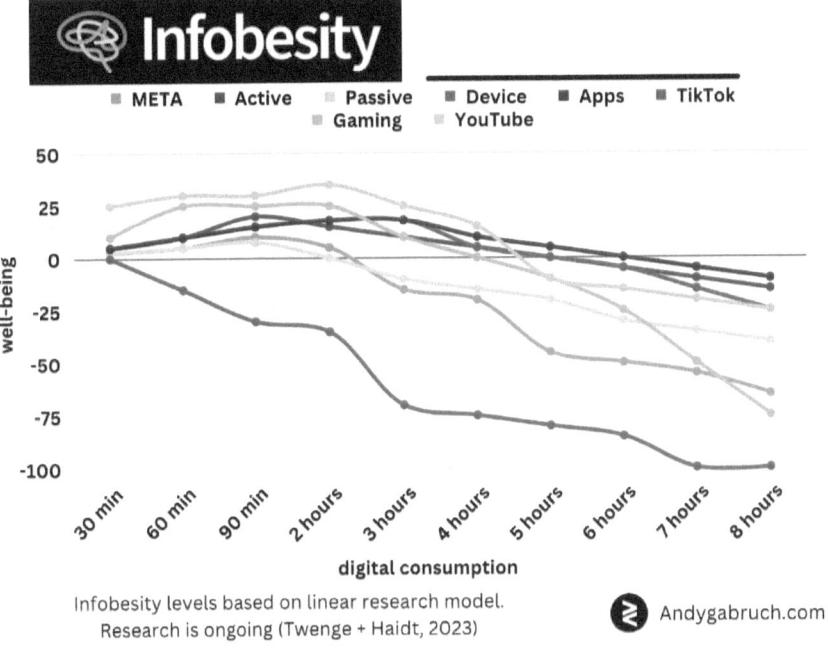

Infobesity levels based on linear research model. Research is ongoing (Twenge + Haidt, 2023)   Andygabruch.com

As you can see, the chart outlines different social media platforms digital users consume. Based on the research gathered from followers of Jesus and nonbelievers alike, those who have engaged in digital usage between thirty minutes to two hours a day results in positive outcomes. This includes connecting with friends, interacting with family, reading the latest news; the results show practical information has a benefit.[4]

However, as you can see with the chart, two hours of digital usage begins a gradual decline of personal well-being of digital users. Depending on the platform and the variable well-being of the participant, you can see the negative effects of *infobesity* increasing over time.

Of course, it made sense for digital users to reject digital platforms due to their negative effects of *infobesity*; and yet, at the same time, there is a great opportunity for followers of Jesus to be redemptive online.

---

4. As mentioned, practical information is a source of information which gives us the ability to understand the "how-to's" of life. This could include how to fix a car or reset your digital device. According to the results of *infobesity* assessments, over 70 percent of participants engage online seeking practical information.

Nevertheless, the opposite is also true. There are digital users who receive digital information with limited digital self-awareness skills. The consequent damage to their personal well-being are experiencing the full affects of the digital trinity.

Receive

Repeatedly, we would hear stories of, "Yes, I know I am addicted (to digital spaces), but I am godly." Digital users recognize their distractions on digital spaces but didn't take redemptive measures to deal with the levels of *infobesity* they are experiencing. Some participants reacted to our research by saying, "Who cares about my digital practices! I am online all the time."[5]

The more we asked participants about their digital practices, we recognized the dissonance between their lack of self-awareness skills to their personal digital habits.

However, as we offered participants redemptive tools to understand the symptoms of *infobesity* they were facing, numerous participants appreciated the resources around the research. We were thanked for the research as it allowed them to address their lack of digital self-awareness skills. We heard comments like, "Thank you for showing us how distracted we are online," to, "I am convicted about my digital practices. Thank you for helping me understand how much time I waste online." For the *infobesity* model we developed, when participants understood their digital practices, then they were empowered to develop self-awareness skills in digital spaces.

Due to this, we created an *infobesity* assessment to empower digital users to build redemptive practices. Instead of rejecting digital spaces or receiving digital spaces with limited personal reflection, we wanted to provide practical tools for followers of Jesus, and non-faith digital users as well, to experience personal well-being living in a digital world.

---

5. Gabruch, "Infobesity," 97.

CHAPTER SIX: WELL-BEING IN AN INFOBESITY WORLD

Receive   Redeem   Reject

The development of the *infobesity* self-assessment is based on Jesus' words as the new SHEMA. The design of the assessment has been personalized for students, parents, pastors, and the general public. We have offered these assessments as resources to provide redemptive digital practices for digital users. In fact, before we go any further, I would like you to go through the *infobesity* self-assessment. It should take no more than five minutes. It is complementary, and is an ongoing resource for you and those closest to you.[6]

OK, so now that you are back from the *infobesity* self-assessment, what level of information overload are you experiencing?

Based on your personal self-assessment on *infobesity*, let me highlight a few redemptive practices which have helped me navigate in a digital world.

2-2-2 Principle

One of the key strategies I have encouraged digital users is to apply the 2-2-2 principle. As mentioned above, the 2-2-2 principle provides a guideline for digital users to shape digital spaces rather than be shaped by digital spaces.

This would include a two-hour digital-free zone when you wake up, a two-hour digital-free zone before you go to bed, and a two-hour limit on social media use per day.

I would encourage you to apply this style of digital activity into your life. Share screenshots of your digital activity using the 2-2-2 principle. Examine where you're spending your time online. Ask yourself, "Has my well-being increased, decreased, or remained the same?" Feel free to write

---

6. You can access the *infobesity* self-assessment at www.andygabruch.com/redeem-digitalspaces. Please use the promo code DUCO or you will be charged.

down your experiences and share with a friend. Has this principle been difficult for you to practice? Why or why not?

Digital-Free Zones

Another key redemptive practice is to create digital-free zones.

Our research on *infobesity* reveals the most harmful digital habits have been practiced in the isolation of a bedroom or bathroom. As a family, we do not allow digital devices in bedrooms or bathrooms because we want our family to develop healthy digital practices. Adolescent women especially have shared the guilt and shame stemming from their private digital practices. The findings are overwhelming from our research. Isolationism, harmful digital practices, and decreased personal well-being increase when digital usage is experienced in private spaces.

In addition to the practices above, we have created digital-free zones in public spaces. This has included the dinner table and car rides to school and back. The reason for this is to foster an environment for intentional and organic conversations to thrive. At our dinner table, for example, anything really goes. In fact, here is a glimpse into one of our family conversations:

> Kid 3: Are we out of quarantine yet?
>
> Kid 1: Nope. It doesn't matter because aliens are coming to earth.
>
> Parent 2: really?
>
> Kid 2: Are aliens angels?
>
> Kid 3: I don't want to die in my ninth year of life!
>
> Kid 1: I think WWIII will happen before aliens.
>
> Kid 3: Don't forget the murderous bees!
>
> Kid 2: I wonder what heaven will be like. Maybe we will be in heaven by the end of the summer.
>
> Kid 4: . . . Keep[s] eating patiently.[7]

---

7. Facebook post, June 5, 2020.

There is so much going on in this conversation! In a matter of moments, really, we had multiple conversations going at the same time. It is organized chaos. It is beautiful.

The dinner table, for example, is a great place to foster healthy relationships. Around the dinner table, social skills are developed. Cognitive reasoning increases: and as you can see from the conversation above, safe conversations are vital to developing personal well-being. Healthy conversations are best fostered face-to-face. Conversations which develop confidence, resiliency, and a sense of belonging. These types of face-to-face conversations we are designed to have are limited on digital spaces.

Digital spaces have a difficulty to offer the benefits of face-to-face conversations. Healthy conversations include nonverbal cues. Healthy conversations, in the experiences of our home, are best fostered organically and unintentionally; and yet, are intentionally enough to thrive.

I'd encourage you to develop digital-free zones in your home. You will see for yourself—healthy digital practices will thrive. You will discover the joys of healthy conversations as you foster safe places beyond digital spaces.

Digital Detox

Last, a redemptive digital practice you can include is a digital detox. A digital detox is a certain amount of time to reset yourself from digital activity. It could be an afternoon or evening, or it can include a full day or weekend, or a series of digital detoxes to monitor your own well-being.

In our research on *infobesity*, we would encourage digital detoxes over rejecting digital platforms. The reason for this, as you can see with the chart above, is that digital practices and habits do have benefits to our personal well-being; especially when digital practices and habits are monitored, regulated, and redeemed.

For some, it might include a break from a smartphone to use of a flip phone. You are still able to be connected with those closest to you through voice and text, but not be as distracted with a smartphone. This is a great option for younger generations. Younger generations have a difficult time discerning their personal digital practices. As their brains are maturing, the enormous amounts of information they are consuming can be harmful. Due to this, rather than being constantly preoccupied by screens, a flip phone is a great alternative.

Another option could be monitoring what type of digital information you are interacting with. As you can see with the chart above, not all digital platforms are the same. There are platforms designed to share hateful and harmful information, and other platforms designed to share helpful and practical information. The level of *infobesity* a digital user experiences is uniquely tied to the digital platform they are engaging in.

Not all digital information is negative or harmful. We just need to moderate digital practices for our own well-being.

Based on the redemptive digital practices mentioned above, how can you start implementing these practices in your life? For me, these strategies became opportunities to shape my relationships, reconnect with the divine, and minimize the digital distractions in a world being shaped by *infobesity*.

Hopefully, it isn't being online twenty-five hours per day.

Personal Reflections

- Based on the *infobesity* self-assessment, what are the top three *infobesity* symptoms you are currently facing?
- Based on the *infobesity* self-assessment, what have you learned about your personal digital practices and habits?
- Do you gravitate to, reject, or receive digital spaces with deficient self-awareness? Why or why not?

CHAPTER SEVEN: Jesus in an Infobesity World

"What is Truth?"
—Pontius Pilate (John 18:38)

"I am the Way, the Truth, and the Life."
—Jesus (John 14:6)

How do you define truth?

The episode of Pilate in John 18:38 is an ironic story about truth.

It is unfortunate historic reality we do not know much about Pontius Pilate. We can speculate, but we have limited knowledge about Pilate before his encounter with Jesus. Even after the trials of Jesus, we do not hear much about Pilate in the history books.

We do know there were underlying factors of tension between the Jewish people and the Roman Empire, but we can only guesstimate at the details.

With this being said, we can assume Pilate had the ability to do what he wanted. He was in a position of power and authority. For example, if he wanted to start a building project with temple money, he could (and probably did). If he wanted to exercise his power over Jewish rebels, he had the power to do so. If he wanted to do something, he had the freedom to exercise his authority.

Essentially, he had the ability to create his own truth.

When he sarcastically asked Jesus, "What is truth?" he did not know he was standing with the One who is ultimately the Truth (John 14:6).

The Bible indicates Pilate wasn't being real with Jesus. He wasn't planning to seek the truth about Jesus or wanted to know the truth. He released Jesus to the religious mobs because he wanted to protect his own truth.[1]

In his own words, he questioned Jesus about his authority and power. He interrogated the religious leaders of their accusations about Jesus. In addition to this, we see the exchanges of power plays between Pilate, the religious elite, the Jewish mobs, and Jesus testifying as the truth (John 18:37).

As an ironic story of power, the games John records in the series of interactions with Pilate, Jesus, and the crowds are played between ultimate authority, strength, and truth. This power play remains the same in digital spaces too. There are rings of power plays of information demanding "their truths" to be heard, to be told, and to be accepted.

We do not need to go far into the digital world to see power plays at work. The reels, the comments, the videos, the shared stories all demand their side of the truth. This is nothing new throughout the history of human dynamics and power. In fact, during Jesus' day, the Roman Empire had their own truth to be governed by. Even the religious leaders had their own truths to be controlled by. And, as the story unfolded with Jesus, Pilate, the mob, and religious leaders, each of them were using their own power and authority to share their own truths to get their own ways. It is a story of truth but it is much deeper than that.

It is a story of authority.

Surprisingly, Jesus doesn't use truth to power play with Pilate or with the religious leaders or to the mob. He simply uncovered the Truth. Ultimately, He reveals the One—who has the final power and authority—to declare what is real and true, not the personalized truths of the culture around us, through his resurrection.

An important reality with truth—truth is testified. In the first century (as we still do today), truth is communicated by an eyewitness—to experience,

---

1. Schwartz, "Pontius Pilate (Person)," 5:399.

CHAPTER SEVEN: JESUS IN AN INFOBESITY WORLD

to mirror, to proof, and to give evidence of an episode or situation.[2] In this case, Jesus came to testify, as an eyewitness, for Truth—the very essence of Truth. He came to reveal Truth in a world of individualistic truths.

This is a phenomenal reality for followers of Jesus. Truth, ultimately, is a person. Jesus is confessing to be the Truth. Truth—whatever aligns with reality—points to a Person. A Person revealing clarity, purpose, and freedom found in the Truth. Not in the personalized truths of confusion and relational frustration. This means Jesus is worthy to submit my truth for his Truth. This is reality.

My reality, as a follower of Jesus, changes when I submit to the Truth found in Jesus. My pursuit of information online with the endless seeking and searching for truth in a digital world leads to futile concepts of truth. In fact, when Jesus confesses he is the Truth, he is inviting you and me to experience a real, truthful God. A God who is Truth, will bring Truth, and reveal Truth to the real world.

Jesus' response to Pilate's ironic question, "What is truth?" is to point to himself as the King of Truth.

He has the final authority. He is the Ultimate Truth. But the story doesn't end there. It gets wild. Before Pilate gives Truth over to the religious mob, they react to Pilate and demand that he kill the King of Truth. They shout at him, "We have no other king than Caesar" (John 19:15).

Really? Caesar?!

They are about to trade the Person of Truth for the cult of the culture around them? Seriously?!

They are about to reject the author of creation for the convenience of what they have created (as their own personal truths). The religious elite manipulated the crowd. They turned them into a powerful mob. They were about to exchange the authority of Truth, as seen in Jesus, for their own religious and personalized truths.

What a sad day!

---

2. *Concise Oxford English Dictionary*, 11th ed., s.v. "eyewitness."

This story is a series of ironic conversations. In fact, this story sounds familiar to the golden calf episode of old, doesn't it? The ancient people of God rejecting the tablets of stone are now rejecting Jesus as the tablets of their hearts.

So often, though, we exchange the Truth for our own truths, don't we? In our digital world today, it seems like we aren't as interested in the Truth as much as following the mobs of personalized truths. And in digital spaces, the mobs online are real.

I have been blasted for sharing my faith.

I have been ridiculed for writing encouraging posts.

I have been bombarded by online hate for not being an expert on what I post.

The online mobs of post-truth rhetoric, tailored truths based on our own entertainment and consumption, and leveraging our own agendas are riddled throughout digital spaces.

I think we have all experienced the onslaught of digital mobs at times. And during the online mobs, we can become distracted by our own truths rather than follow the Truth of Jesus.

Brett McCracken, in his latest book *The Wisdom Pyramid*, suggests, "In today's post-truth world, 'facts' are seen as fluid, bias laden things to dispute or ignore when they threaten us."[3] Due to this, our focus in digital spaces lean to filtering information not based on the Truth of Jesus but based on our own personal experiences, feelings, and relationships.

Oddly, in a world of personalized truth, submitting to the Truth is the healthiest way to combat *infobesity*. The levels of misinformation, disinformation, hateful, and harmful information affecting the well-being of digital users is not only experienced through redemptive practices from the Truth but allowing the Truth to guide us in a world of personalized truths.

So, we need to ask ourselves, not as Pilates asked, but to genuinely ask Jesus, "What is truth?"

---

3. McCracken, *Wisdom Pyramid*, 50.

In Pilate's encountered, he did not recognize Truth as a Person. For Pilate, truth is subjective. Truth is based on a stream of facts or modified opinions. Yet, Truth is deeper than the digital influences of hypersensitive and individualistic mobs found in digital spaces. Truth is more than a series of experiences validating our feelings or alternated facts of digitalized processes.

Throughout history, philosophers have wrestled with the questions of truth. For many philosophers, simply put, truth is whatever lines up with reality. Reality accepts how things are. The best way I can put it is that reality lines up with real life.

For the concepts of truth to be encountered in a world bombarded by *infobesity*, truth is deeper than personal information, agendas, and feelings. Truth is experienced. Truth is encountered. Truth admits reality.

For Jesus, he reveals Truth. He is Truth.

He came to show us the way to Truth.

In Mark 6:3 and Matthew 13:55, we see Jesus is portrayed as a "carpenter." The word "carpenter" comes from the Greek word "tekton," which gives us the modern-day word "technology." In addition to this, the word "tekton," in the original language, means more than the English definition of a carpenter. The word tekton would include the description of a builder, a mason, or someone who builds with their hands.

In the context of truth, Jesus built more than homes. He built the universe. He spoke the cosmos into being. He provided order where there was chaos. He spoke light into the darkness.

In the beginning, we see God spoke creation into being.[4] The earth was chaotic, formless, empty, and dark, and yet he spoke order, purpose, life, and light into the world. This is the creation story.

In the creation story, truth was given form. Truth brought order, purpose, life, and light into the world. The cosmos was formed. The Truth breathed humanity into being, speaking truth, purpose, and relationship into humanity.

---

4. In Genesis 1, the creative work of God was to "speak" Creation into being. Ten times, the Scriptures indicate "God said" (Gen 1:3, 6, 9, 11, 14, 20, 24, and the pinnacle of the Creation story of "speaking" humanity into being in Gen 1:26, 28, 29).

PART TWO: RESPONDING TO INFOBESITY AS FOLLOWERS OF JESUS

In the fullness of time, Jesus revealed Truth in human form. He took on the burden of sin and brokenness from creation.[5] Through the Personhood of Jesus, he is now revealing truth through new creations. The apostle Paul, an early church leader in the first century, gives much attention to this. In fact, to a confused and struggling church experiencing ancient forms of *infobesity* in Corinth, he shares the truth this way: "Anyone in Christ Jesus is now a new creation in Christ Jesus" (2 Cor 5:17). As followers of Jesus, we are now new creations in him.

He speaks of a new reality in us, for us, and through us. We are now not distracted by modern-day *infobesity* of digital spaces and places but are breathed into purpose by the divine Tekton.

Amazingly enough, it is the same divine Tekton who created the heavens and the earth who also created technology. Jesus is known as the ultimate techie! Due to this, we do not need to reject digital spaces or receive digital spaces with unlimited consumption, but we can invite Jesus into our digital spaces and places as the divine Tekton.

Paradoxically, however, the rise of technology in our world has developed a concept called technicism.

Technicism is the philosophy in which all of humanity's problems can be solved through technology. The positive outcomes of technicism in the last one hundred years have increased the quality of life. This has included medicine, modern-day sciences, and modes of communication which have had revolutionary results on the world. Technicism has advanced and increased efficiency and productivity. However, technicism has left us disappointed. Technicism is limited to answer the deeper questions of humanity.

For instance, we are still deeply lonely. We are marked by mental ill-being as a society. Symptomatically, we are wrestling with modern-day forms of *infobesity*. So, in our own forms of truth rather than following the Truth, technicism is exploring how to combat *infobesity*, for example, with personalized relationships in the form of humanlike robots.[6]

Just like the ancient selfie of Exodus 32 and the debacle of the golden calf episode, it is the human condition to try to find our own answers to our

---

5. We touched on this as he effects of living in the digital garden in chapter 3.
6. See "AI Expert David Levy."

selfish questions. We would rather have a relationship with a humanlike robot than submit to the Truth of Jesus. Even in the digital garden, Adam and Eve's pursuit for information was more important to them than Truth. Due to this, we have never truly reached our full potential and our purpose in life. We surround ourselves with our own technology rather than Jesus as Tekton.

As we have journeyed throughout these pages together, there are only questions the divine Tekton can answer. In the Gospel of John, Jesus provides the answer.

At the beginning of time, Jesus is the One who has defined reality. It is Jesus who has become the Truth for humanity. In fact, Jesus himself is reality. And this renewed reality is experienced through his redemptive work.

This gives us great hope. We can allow Jesus to renew our digital practices and habits by experiencing his truth, hope, love, and helpful information rather than modern-day forms of *infobesity*.

If we invite Jesus into our digital spaces, he will become the filter of how to process modern-day *infobesity*. We can trust in Jesus because he is the ultimate techie!

Due to this, Jesus is more than some digital trinket!

Jesus is God. In actuality, Jesus is better than a golden calf or a modern-day technological trinket. He is better than the latest video game or digital upgrade. He is better than the latest tech gadget. He is better than high-speed internet and free Wi-Fi (yes, this is true!). Jesus is better because he leads us to truth.

When defining truth as reality, Jesus reveals an amazing opportunity to encounter truth. Truth isn't just a Person. Truth becomes relational. Jesus doesn't manipulate truth with online agenda-based information. He doesn't bombard you and me with online cheap entertainment. He doesn't distract you and me with the pings, bings, and dings from digital devices. He foundationally offers you and me a divine relationship.

You might have never heard why truth is relational; however, relational truth is a reality because of His love for us. In all the religions and spiritual practices in the world today,[7] Jesus is the only person who offers a divine relationship based on love. His love is not based on human achievements or performance. He offers a relational truth unmatched by any digital relationship or information we pursue.

Due to this, Jesus combats all forms, experiences, and aspects of *infobesity*. He answers the modern-day loneliness epidemic[8] with purpose. He answers the pursuit of endless online information with divine truth and clarity.

He fulfills the deepest questions of identity, formation, and well-being.

It is quite amazing. The divine outwitting the digital. Jesus offers relationships like no other.

In digital spaces, followers of Jesus have the unique reality to invite Jesus into digital places. We can allow Jesus to shape our digital practices and habits as we enter digital spaces and places with the divine Tekton in relational Truth.

As followers of Jesus, we can live in the light of the Truth of Jesus in a digital world. What great hope!

Jesus is the ultimate tablet!

An early church follower of Jesus named Paul, an early church leader, wrote how Jesus is the ultimate tablet. Listen to how the apostle Paul puts it:

> Your lives are a letter written in our hearts; everyone can read it and recognize our good work among you. Clearly, you are a letter from Christ showing the result of our ministry among you. This "letter" is written not with pen and ink, but with the Spirit of the living God. It is carved not on tablets of stone, but on human hearts. (2 Cor 3:2–3 NLT)

Paul is referring to Exodus 32. He is quoting the ancient selfie story. He is contrasting the tablets of stone from the golden calf disaster with the

---

7. There are roughly thirty-three thousand different religions and spiritual organizations in the world today. Only Jesus reveals a divine relationship based on grace rather than works or performance or higher spiritual learning. This is ultimately, the *best* reality we have as followers of Jesus.

8. OSG, *Our Epidemic of Loneliness and Isolation*.

CHAPTER SEVEN: JESUS IN AN INFOBESITY WORLD

tablets written on the human heart.⁹ As the divine Tekton to humanity and the relational Truth for humanity, no earthly advancement or achievement could take the place of the divine needs of the human soul like Jesus. No man-made, high-pressure glass with glowing and addictive flashing screen tablets can satisfy the tablets of our own hearts like Jesus.

Jesus as relational. Truth as relational. Jesus as powerful. Truth which is transformational. Jesus comes to reveal the truth to heal, set free, and download purpose into our lives living in an *infobesity* world.

This begs the question for you and me—who live, eat, breathe, work, communicate, and interact in digital spaces—is Jesus the Truth we filter and discern our digital spaces?

If Truth resides in us, as followers of Jesus, then the divinity of Jesus provides a better way of how to overcome *infobesity* in the digital world we live in.

Just like the ancient stories of the digital garden and the golden calf, Jesus reveals a *new* way of life in a technological world. I call this reality a technological "Way of Life."¹⁰ Jesus invites you and me to apply the divine truths of Tekton to our digital practices.

In my own life, with my family of two teenagers and two preteens, we invited Jesus into our digital worlds. For us, it is an opportunity to develop a technology "Way of Life." It allows Jesus to speak truth into our digital practices.

Regulate Digital Devices

The first thing we did as a family was to moderate and regulate digital devices. In my research on *infobesity* with parents, students, and children, I recognized the need for digital boundaries for those who have become digitalized since the pandemic. This included the following strategies:

---

9. See Exod 24:12; 31:18; 32:15; 34:1; Deut 9:10.

10. You can download the technology "Way of Life" at www.infobesity.ca or find the template in the resource section of the book.

PART TWO: RESPONDING TO INFOBESITY AS FOLLOWERS OF JESUS

Children (Ages 2-9)

For children between the ages of two and nine years, we recommend:

- Limiting digital consumption to thirty minutes to two hours a day (excluding school),
- Digital devices are always in public spaces (in the home),
- No social media platforms,
- Monitoring digital consumption by parents for videos, or gaming, or connecting with family and friends,
- Educating your children on digital spaces and places, and
- Practice weekly digital sabbaths as a family.

Preteens (Ages 10-12)

For children ages between ten and twelve years old, we recommend:

- Limiting digital consumption to two hours a day (excluding school),
- Developing a rule of technology for your children,
- No social media platforms (as social media platforms prohibit children under thirteen; unless parents are monitoring those platforms),
- No personal digital devices (family devices only),
- Using parental settings on all devices,
- Creating a "fun list" with your children,
- Educating your preteens on the harmful effects of digital spaces and places, and
- Practicing weekly digital sabbaths as a family.

Teenagers (Ages 13-19)

And for teenagers between thirteen and eighteen, we recommend:

- Moderating digital consumption to two hours a day (excluding school and work),

- Developing a personal plan with your child on the rule of technology and a "fun list" for non-screen activities,
- Creating weekly digital-free spaces and places for friends and conversations to thrive,
- Sharing peer and/or family stories on the realities of information overload, and
- Practicing weekly digital sabbaths with your teens.

Young Adults (Ages 20–25)

For young adults, who consider digital spaces as important as the air they breathe and the food they eat, we recommend:

- Limiting social media consumption to two hours a day (excluding work and education),
- Developing a personal technology "Way of Life," and
- Discerning how to build a Jesus brand online (rather than your own brand).[11]

Adults (Ages 25+)

For adults, as digital pilgrims,[12] we recommend:

- Limiting social media consumption to two hours a day (excluding work and education). This includes news reels and active or passive scrolling;
- Developing a personal technology "Way of Life." When you do this, you lead by example for your family, spouse, and children. As Josh McDowell, a mentor of mine, once said, "Rules without relationship lead to rebellion." This includes leading by example when it comes to our digital consumption and habits in the home.

---

11. We will be exploring in detail how to build a Jesus brand in digital spaces in chapters 10–11.

12. This term refers to the concept of those who were introduced to digital spaces and places in their young adult years. Digital natives, however, are those who were born into digital spaces and places.

- Discerning and develop a Jesus brand online (within your own digital branding).

Digital Detox

In addition to this, we tried digital detoxes in our home. This was a tough one. We slowly started with an afternoon, then added evening, and then a day. Surprisingly enough, it gave us the opportunity to provide a better "yes" for our family rather than being glued to digital spaces. This included digital-free activities, digital-free zones, regulating digital devices, and introducing redemptive practices as a family.

In fact, not only did I experiment with combating modern-day *infobesity* with my family,[13] I was able to apply the principles above with individuals, students, parents, and their families all across the country. In fact, throughout this book, the goal of the stories, practices, latest social sciences, and research described is designed for you to create your own technological "Way of Life." It is an opportunity to combat personal *infobesity* and experience the well-being of Jesus' words in Mark 12:30-31.

If Truth truly resides in us, then the divine is designed to shape us. If Truth is meant to transform us, then the divine Tekton is more important than technicism. We don't need to follow the tablets of old or to be led by the flashing lights of the high-pressure, modern-day tablets of this world. As followers of Jesus, we are to submit to the authority of the One who is Tekton, who is Truth, who is relational, the One who satisfies the tablets of our hearts.

Personal Reflection

- Which redemptive practices could you start implementing in your life, your home, and key relationships?
- How can you start a technological "Way of Life"?
- How can you create a better "yes" to say no to the digital distractions around you?

13. This included hundreds of participants through the *infobesity* self-assessment, various feedback loops, and speaking engagements, the practices presented are the best practices we developed to combat modern-day *infobesity*.

CHAPTER EIGHT: Truth as a Person in a Post-Truth World

"Truth is Beauty, truth beauty,—that is all Ye know on earth, and all ye need to know."
—John Keats[1]

"Knowledge puffs up while love builds up."
—Apostle Paul (1 Cor 8:1)

In a world constantly connected to different forms of information, the only way to sift through digital information is with the truth.[2]

As we have discovered in the previous chapter, Truth is more than a bunch of abstract concepts or empirical learnings or personalized experiences (even though these modes of truth are beneficial), the deepest mode of Truth is a Person. Truth leads to a Person. Truth is love. Truth is relational.

As you and I are created to search truth, the basic form of truth is to seek information. Seeking information is the foundation to discovering knowledge. And knowledge is the capacity to apply information to our lives. As we are wired to seek information, we are designed to practice

---

1. Keats, *Collected Poems*, 67. "Ode on a Grecian Urn" is perhaps the most famous of his five Odes which he composed in 1819.

2. And yet, "the Bible does not provide a systematic account of the nature of truth in either its theological or philosophical dimensions. Nevertheless, great prominence is given to the idea of truth in Scripture because God is the God of truth (Pss 31:5; 108:4; 146:6) who speaks and judges truly (Pss 57:3; 96:13). God is the God of all truth because he is the Creator, and it is impossible for him to lie (Heb 6:18)" (Elwell, *Baker Encyclopedia of the Bible*, 2:2108 [s.v. "truth"]).

truth as we experience knowledge throughout our experiences. Yet, digital information—even forms of helpful information and practical knowledge—experienced in digital spaces and places, is meant to hook you. Information, in digital spaces, is a form of selling. Digital information is a strategy to grab our attention, and in most cases, can lead to empty and useless information. This may create an online information vacuum where information is shared but does not lead to knowledge or truth and has the capacity to harm us rather than help us. This can hinder us from the created well-being Jesus desires us to live.

The Bible calls this type of information empty chatter (1 Tim 6:20), irrelevant babble (2 Tim 2:16), and foolish controversies (Titus 3:9). To the early church, such information led to ungodliness, unprofitable thinking, and worthless forms of knowledge. A fake knowledge distracting followers of Jesus from their God-given fruitfulness. This type of information was not meant to build each other up but to tear each other down in the early church community.

You see, the early church, just like the digital garden and the ancient selfie, struggled with their own forms of *infobesity*. The first-century Christians combatted forms of early church *infobesity* by "walking in the truth" (2 John 4).

Walking in the truth was living out the life-giving commandments of Jesus. For example, John pointed his readers to the words of Jesus in the upper room (John 14–17). This scene is where Jesus revealed truth, once again, in the context of love for God. He told his disciples, "If you love me, you will obey my commands" (John 14:15). In other words, Jesus is saying, "If you love the Truth, you will follow me. If you love me, you will submit to the Truth. If you love me and submit to the Truth, you will obey my commands."

Truth is meant to be practiced.

In our modern-day world, information is dirt cheap. Information is free. Information is easy. Information is effortlessly accessible. Yet, there are other forms of information designed to be transformational. Meant to bring purpose, clarity, and healing in our lives. As modern-day disciples, we may treat all forms of information as digital rather than divine. This includes treating the commands of Jesus as cheap and meaningless rather than true

CHAPTER EIGHT: TRUTH AS A PERSON IN A POST-TRUTH WORLD

and purposeful. This is the difference between thriving and surviving as digital disciples of Jesus. To combat modern-day forms of *infobesity*, we are meant to practice the ways of Jesus. Not only did Jesus reveal the Truth, but he is became the Way, and the Life (John 14:16). To practice the ways of Jesus in a world of *infobesity* is to walk in his truth.

But how do modern-day disciples filter through the enormous amounts and countless types of information we are presented in digital spaces each and every day with truth?

By following the commands of Jesus.

Another way to look at this reality is to live incarnationally with Jesus.

Incarnational living is a fancy way of saying Jesus lives in us (Acts 1:8). Just as Jesus revealed God in human form, Christians have the unique reality of Jesus living in us through the Holy Spirit. The Holy Spirit is always active, living in us twenty-five hours per day. The Holy Spirit divinely connects us with Jesus in a world always digitally connected. Being digitally "on" means we are one to three clicks away from being connected, twenty-five hours per day, to anything, any place, at any time in digital spaces.

Yet, Jesus provides us with tools to live incarnationally, even in a digital world. It is the reality of Jesus being the Way, the Truth, and the Life in our lives.

As Jesus is the Way, we need to ask ourselves, "Does the information I create and the content I interact with online point people to Jesus?" If the answer is "no" or "maybe," then we should respond redemptively and allow Jesus into our digital activity.

Another question we can ask ourselves is, "Are my digital practices leading people closer to Jesus or pushing them further away?" Again, this is a great question, and an opportunity to invite Jesus into our digital worlds. Is Jesus present?

Another compelling way we can filter through online information is through the Truth of who God is. This allows his character to shape our digital practices. Being online is not only about being entertained by the digital trinity or being bombarded with the effects of *infobesity*; it can also reveal the Truth of Jesus. A great reality as followers of Jesus living in a digital world is we can reveal Jesus to others who are experiencing *infobesity*. A great question to ask ourselves is if our digital practices are revealing Jesus to others online.[3]

Another way we can incarnationally engage with online information is as an opportunity to experience life. As Jesus is life, we need to ask ourselves, "Does my online activity encourage godly engagement? Does the information I am about to interact with benefit me as a follower of Jesus? Does the information I am sharing spur people to godly living or plant seeds of doubt?"

These questions of living like Jesus online will help guide us. We can become agents of renewal and redemption in a world experiencing *infobesity*. The filtering system of Jesus as the Way, the Truth, and the Life can become an incarnational practice with our digital activity.

It is interesting to note, no one on earth has ever described themselves as the Way, the Truth, and the Life like Jesus. This statement has become the fundamental reality of how to follow Jesus. Jesus reveals he is the SHEMA, a statement of Jesus' divinity empowering his followers to navigate through modern forms of *infobesity* you and I are experiencing.

What great hope we have as followers of Jesus.

But there is still another important reality for followers of Jesus when it comes to combating modern-day *infobesity*. It is the reality of the Holy Spirit living in and through us.

Jesus describes the Holy Spirit to his closest friends as the "Spirit of Truth" (John 16:13; 14:26). This means Jesus equips Christians with the Holy Spirit to discern what is godly, right, and true. The Holy Spirit is an ongoing relational resource to filter *infobesity* through the Truth of Jesus. The Spirit teaches us and reminds us how to practically live in the Truth in everyday life.

This isn't just a unique reality of living incarnationally with the Way, the Truth, and the Life of Jesus but the Spirit who empowers his followers to communicate to the world.[4]

---

3. We will discuss how to reveal Jesus in digital spaces in section three of the book.
4. Morris, *Gospel According to John*, 577.

CHAPTER EIGHT: TRUTH AS A PERSON IN A POST-TRUTH WORLD

What a great resource God gives us! We can encounter truth and find inspiration through the Holy Spirit! The Holy Spirit is with us. The Holy Spirit guides us. The Holy Spirit reminds us how to be like followers of Jesus online.

And yet, there is still one more reality we as followers of Jesus must face to combat modern-day *infobesity*. To the early church, the words of Jesus were not just experienced Truth through a Person or through the Spirit of Truth but through the Word of God. A church leader put it this way to a young apprentice:

> All Scripture is inspired by God and is useful to teach us what is true and to make us realize what is wrong in our lives. It corrects us when we are wrong and teaches us to do what is right. God uses it to prepare and equip his people to do every good work. (2 Tim 3:16–17 NLT)

The Word of God is a great resource to overcome modern-day *infobesity*. Scripture is more than words on paper. The Word has the power to lead us to all Truth. Through the Scriptures, we can encounter the Truth of Jesus. Through the pages of the Bible, we get to experience God! This is through personal and general revelation to you and me.

Revelation is a theological term where truth is revealed to us through Jesus, the Holy Spirit, and the Scriptures. For me, there have been so many times I have been reading the Scriptures and the words seem to jump off the pages. The words become life to me as the Scriptures enter my mind and heart. It is like a surprise narrative—the Word sinks deep into me, surprising me with the revelational Truth of Jesus. At times, the Scriptures have encouraged me. Other times, the Scriptures have pointed me to a godly perspective. In various seasons of my life, the Scriptures were life-giving to me, offering me hope and peace. Truth, through the Scriptures, reveals Jesus to us! When we apply the Scriptures to them, our lives can be transformed.

In addition to this, his Word has the power—through the Holy Spirit—to sift through the lies we interact with, especially the information we consume online. The Scriptures have the power to protect us. The Scriptures can help us filter through the voices of hurtful comments and guide us on how to redemptively respond. The Scriptures encourage us in the midst of the burdens we see in digital spaces. His Word has the power to heal our souls. The Word can mend our minds. His Word can realign our hearts when we are out of sorts. The Scriptures reveal the nature of God and grants us peace when we are overwhelmed with an overabundance of information.

The Scriptures invite us to experience God. When we do experience God through the Scriptures, the Scriptures have the power to shape us to be more like Jesus rather than be manipulated by our socials.

The Scriptures have the unique ability to reach out to us personally. God's Word is not just a dusty science textbook or a crusty math quiz. His Word is not nasty or out-of-date or crazy (even though there are some crazy stories in it). But the Bible is uniquely designed to empower you with purpose—speaking the reality of Jesus as Truth in your life.

How is your relationship with the Word? How can the Bible help you in an infobese world?

As an example, early church believers would interact with the Scriptures *with* each other. Once a week, followers of Jesus would gather around a table for a meal and to discuss Scripture. Believe it or not, the Scriptures are not designed to be read in private. The Bible was meant to be interacted with in relationships.

Church members in the first century would gather in homes to hear the Word of God. In some settings, the Scriptures would be read by a church leader and then discussed with everyone over lunch. This gave time for followers of Jesus to ask questions about what they had heard and how to apply the Scriptures to their lives that week. Together, over a meal, they would pray with one another and encourage one another to practice the commandments of Jesus in their lives.

Personally, I am so thankful for having relationships in my life that have pointed me to the Scriptures. There have been times in my life where I have been discouraged. There have been moments where I have felt deflated and burdened. And yet, in those moments, friends would gather and pray for me. My local church would encourage me. They would love me.

It is a beautiful picture when the Truth of Jesus is personally experienced. It is life-changing. It is an amazing reality to be strengthened and encouraged by fellow followers of Jesus and to put into practice the Way of Jesus for those around me.

CHAPTER EIGHT: TRUTH AS A PERSON IN A POST-TRUTH WORLD

The Bible is not designed to be read and interpreted individually. The Bible is meant to be shared in community and practiced through our relationships.

So often, I have heard how difficult it is for modern-day followers of Jesus to read the Scriptures. Busyness, misunderstanding, and not knowing where to start has been the thematic in people's responses to the Scriptures. Still, when we do read the Scriptures, interact with the Scriptures, and apply the Scriptures in community as the early church did, the Word becomes rich and alive.

As a pastor, I encourage people to read the Word in community. Whether it is at a coffee house or a Sunday morning context before or after church services, gathering to go through the Scriptures can be a life-changing practice. The Scriptures become interactive in community. The Word becomes practical in relationships. The Scriptures are applied in community.

The Scriptures become fresh and alive in our lives.

With the number of options of how to interact with the Scriptures in our modern-day world through digital apps, online videos, channels, and reading platforms, it is amazing how many ways we can interact with the Bible. Yet biblical illiteracy continues to increase.[5] In fact, the latest data links biblical illiteracy to modern-day distractions of *infobesity*. We are too busy or too preoccupied or too scared to get into the Word. I encourage you to combat the digital distractions of our modern-day times, why not try to apply the Scriptures to be read, applied, and practiced in community. Why not gather with a few of your friends, classmates, or family members to go through the Scriptures together over a meal or a coffee or a Slurpee. If you want to combat *infobesity* and find well-being through the SHEMA, then reading the Truth of Scripture with one another. It will be a life-giving practice!

As we continue to journey through a world of personalized truth and hyper-individualism, the way to combat modern-day *infobesity* is through the Person of Truth. His name is Jesus.

He gives us the tools through the power of the Holy Spirit and the divine transformational truths of Scripture to be applied in relational contexts.

---

5. Hawkins, "Nation's Biblical Illiteracy."

When we do, we are empowered to live in the Way, the Truth, and the Life in our infobese world.

Personal Reflection

- Have you found *infobesity* shape you more than the Savior? How or how not?
- How can you combat modern-day *infobesity* with the Truth, the Way, and the Life?
- Out of the modes of Truth as a Person, Spirit, Scripture, and church community, which one will you implement in your life? Share a story at www.infobesity.ca.

CHAPTER NINE: Community in an Infobesity World

"As iron sharpens iron, one person sharpens another."
—King Solomon (Prov 27:17)

"A new command I give to you: Love one another."
—Jesus (John 13:34)

Every year, there seems to be a craze for the release of the latest and greatest tech gadget. People wait countless of hours in long lines just to get their hands on the shiny stuff. It is like we get sucked into the craze, spending hundreds, if not thousands of dollars, on personal technology.

It can be the most recent state-of-the-art digital device. It can be a brand new game. It can be downloading the newest (and hottest) social media app. Whatever it is, we get distracted by the latest and greatest tech.

The recurring problem with the digital trinity is when we get bored with easy entertainment, we search for forms of the latest and greatest fix. I call it the entertainment trap. Rather than innovate or cope with boredom in creative ways, we default to what is easy and cheap.

When we chase after the latest and greatest, we chase after our own feedback loops. We chase after personal happiness. We chase after dopamine fixes. When we chase an experience rather than relationships, we get caught up in our own entertainment cycles.

Modern-day counselors and psychologists have linked the phenomenon of digital entertainment to social anxiety.

The irony is that social anxiety has resulted in personalized feedback loops for digital entertainment. For example, we compare ourselves with digital influencers for entertainment. We compete for followers or engagements or likes and comments on digital platforms as entertainers. We pursue the latest and greatest forms of entertainment to consume. And, innately, we feel we are not good enough because we are trapped by entertainment, to be entertained, and to entertain.

Higher forms of digital entertainment can cause social fears. We fear people. We fear what people would think of us, online and offline. We fear social and digital rejection.

These are all signs of social *infobesity*.

In these vulnerable moments, we can compromise our values. We can question our personal integrity. Personalized feedback loops tend to offer shallow hope and instant gratification. Cheap entertainment offers small hits of dopamine, as we portray our digital selves better than our real selves.

Think of all the filters on social media platforms. We can display ourselves however we want even though it creates pseudo forms of ourselves rather than who we really are.

Consider a study published in the journal *Body Image*. Surveying over seven hundred adolescents between ten and eighteen, and university students between ages nineteen and twenty-five, the study revealed even those with moderate digital consumption wrestle with social anxiety.[1] Based on the analysis, those who have experienced increased levels of digital consumption struggle with higher levels of social comparison. Even though the consumption of digital platforms is for entertainment purposes, users faced anxiety, physical comparison, fears of rejection, and consequently developed a hypersensitive personal sense of isolationism.

I think we have all experienced social anxiety in digital spaces. A sign of the entertainment trap is that we tend to isolate ourselves from face-to-face relationships and are more comfortable having digital conversations

---

1. Hawes et al., "Social Media Use," 67–77.

instead. Have you ever noticed yourself developing a digital entertainment loop with your family or friends?

For me, there have been times where I have caught myself mindlessly scrolling through digital information and have noticed how much time I have wasted watching news reels or funny cat videos or some political post. I have had to develop boundaries around my digital activity simply because I was being caught in the entertainment loop.

Another report highlighted in *Psychiatric Quarterly*[2] examined 467 young adults. Based on this research, the study concluded that moderate to higher levels of digital consumption were linked to modern-day loneliness, decreased empathy in key relationships, and amplified negative mental health symptoms. The report included self-destructive ideation and further levels of social isolationism as users increased their digital entertainment activity patterns. In fact, the younger the digital user, the greater the risk of experiencing anxiety was.[3]

According to another study from *Maclean's* magazine on "digital zombies," low usage of social media (between ten minutes to one hour per day) resulted in positive interactions developing for digital users. Those between the ages of twelve to fourteen had healthy outcomes from this level of digital consumption. Nevertheless, moderate to high levels (between one hour to five hours) of social media consumption had the opposite effect. In this study, social anxiety was found to affect not only key relationships at school with friends and teachers, but to also negatively affected relationships with parents and family members.[4] In conclusion, digital entertainment was isolating users from each other.

As a longtime youth pastor, and as a parent of four emerging adolescents, I have seen the effects of *infobesity* in my family, the young people I have shepherded, their families, and in myself.

For instance, I have had parents connect with me after an *Infobesity* session confessing they had to lock their children's digital devices in the family safe because their children were tired and cranky in the mornings before

---

2. Berryman et al., "Social Media Use."
3. Rapee et al., "Risk for Social Anxiety."
4. See Rinaldi, "They Lost Their Kids to *Fortnite*."

school. In their search for why, they found out their children were getting up in the middle of the night to play video games on their devices.

I have seen students self-sabotage their well-being, their grades, and their family value systems because of their digital consumption, their desire to be entertained and to entertain. To these students, their digital practices and habits were justified as they searched for meaningful relationships online. To them, their digital practices were called for in the hope for a new family—a digital family. In addition to this, I have experienced parents deny their own negative digital practices and habits. Even though they have recognized their digital addictions, they felt their digital practices weren't affecting their homes in negative ways. It is like they were in some sort of digital denial.

I have counseled hundreds of students, parents, and families who have been gripped with the deep pains of shame and guilt based of their online practices. I have spoken at conferences, camps, and workshops on *infobesity* across the world. I have experienced the ongoing frustration of parents who feel stuck on how to navigate their children living in a digital age.

In reflection, I have had people respond to my presentations with praise or pain. People would praise the redemptive practices. Families would tell me they have experienced hope on how to deal with digital addiction in their homes. However, the opposite is also true. I have had students heckle me to defend their digital devices. I have had people push back at me because their digital practices were extremely important to them. In addition to this, others were shocked by how much time they have spent in digital spaces. To them, no one had asked them about their digital practices and habits before. It is like we have become digitalized as individuals, families, and as a society.

The truth of digital consumption is a daily reminder of how important it is to manage our own well-being. Modern-day forms of *infobesity* are for real.

For example, in response to the growth of social isolationism in England, the United Kingdom conducted a study with ten thousand volunteers monitoring the levels of loneliness in their citizens. Modern-day loneliness decreased by 84 percent when people served the needs of others. In addition to this, feelings of community increased by 66 percent.[5]

5. Relationships ANSW, "What Is Chronic Loneliness?," para. 17.

CHAPTER NINE: COMMUNITY IN AN INFOBESITY WORLD

Amazing, right? It is like we are hardwired to find purpose, meaning, and significance in relationships.

Interestingly enough, there could be a case made for the decreased levels of church attendance as a significant cause of social infrastructures softening in society.

The context of living in meaningful communities of faith is uniquely tied to the social well-being of any society. As humans, we are designed to be social creatures. We thrive in relationships. We grow in meaning and significance when we serve one another. Our purpose becomes clear. We become increasingly happy when we invite others into our lives. In fact, dopamine levels increase when life is more about others rather than about us and our cheap forms of entertainment.

According to David Levitin, a Canadian neuroscientist and counselor, our quality of life is closely related to the quality of relationships in our lives.[6] People live longer in relationships. People experience personal resiliency in social constructs. People are happier, wealthier, and healthier when they live for other people. Perhaps the modern-day studies and sciences of the benefits of social relationships is why Jesus created the church.

The church is important.

In essence, the church is meant to be a community. The church is on mission for people. Not religion or personal preference, but to have meaningful relationships with each other on mission.

In fact, when you think about it, the church has the opportunity to be the best place to be on planet earth. Only in the church can everyone from any place, from any background, can gather to build relationships with one another.

This reminds me of a small group I led where a PhD student in mathematics, a legal assistant, a high-level executive, and two single moms could gather to pray for one another, encourage one another, and serve together in biblical community. This is only possible because of Jesus. He is the one who brings you and me together (even though we may not know each other).

---

6. Levitin, *Successful Aging*, 199.

PART TWO: RESPONDING TO INFOBESITY AS FOLLOWERS OF JESUS

It is a beautiful picture when the church works correctly. People from every background, context, and with different stories, ranging from various age demographics and ethnic groups, can serve one another because of Jesus.

In fact, because of Jesus, we belong to each other.

One day, we will be together in paradise. It is because of this heavenly reality that we are invited to encourage one another on earth. You might be asking yourself, "Well, how do we practically do this? How can the church be the best place on earth?"

Well, we do this through practicing the "one another" commandments of Jesus. When we practice the one another commandments in the Bible, the church works correctly and community thrives. Relationships are fostered. Collective wisdom is shared. People find meaning. People experience belonging. People protect each other. Truth is practiced. And, in the context of biblical community, people can combat the ever-increasing dangers of modern-day *infobesity* caused in digital spaces.

At the very beginning, God created humanity for community. He created Adam and Eve for God and for each other. From the beginning, the human story of relationships are essential. Relationships help us to process, discern, and decipher information and point towards truth.

In the New Testament context, for example, there are 97 "one another" commandments of Jesus.[7] When the church practiced the one another commandments of Jesus,[8] the church grew in spiritual maturity. As you read the New Testament letters, you will see that 194 times the early church writers challenged their readers how to love each other. This would include sharing resources with those in need. How to show compassion for one another. How to speak truth and love with each other in kindness and reconciliation.

The early church practiced how *not* to gossip. The church encouraged followers of Jesus not to fight with one another, but to lift each other up. They were encouraged to pray for one another and practically help carry each other's burdens. The early church was told not to become easily offended.

---

7. See Kranz, "All the 'One Another' Commands in the NT."

8. In the Sermon on the Mount (Matt 5–7), this famous message became the foundation for the "one another commandments" littered throughout the New Testament.

CHAPTER NINE: COMMUNITY IN AN INFOBESITY WORLD

They were asked to take a higher road and to redeem personal conflict with maturity and grace. Even James, the brother of Jesus, noted loving one another is like being in the presence of royalty. James is saying when we practice the one another commandments of Jesus, we are participating at the hands and feet of the royalty of the glorified Jesus (James 2:8).

It is clear to note Christian maturity in the early church was not linked to the duration of one's faith, but how they treated one another. Jesus put it this way: Christian maturity in the world is based on how we treat one another (John 13:35). The "one another" commandments are not only for communal practice, but are also an evangelistic opportunity to the world around them.

In the same way, the communal reality as a follower of Jesus to combat modern-day *infobesity* is divinely linked to Christ-centered relationships. The church is another key aspect to overcoming *infobesity* in a secular, lonely, individualistic, and ill-being world.

As we see throughout the pages of Truth, these commandments are to "stir up one another to love and good works" (Heb 10:24). It is in these commandments where intentional growth, personal transformation, and strengthened faith are developed. It is the practice of community that "helps us see our blind spots, and areas of needed growth; a diverse community of walking, talking, living examples of Christlikeness we can observe and emulate."[9]

However, in our post-truth age, where ultimate authority has been personalized, the individual has become the primary source of truth. This concept of "self-love" makes following our hearts more important than to "love Christ" by following Christ's command to "love others." The reality of living out "your truth" is more significant than living out the Truth in Jesus. The individualism of our world can even seep into our churches.

However, the context to seek and find relationships based on our own needs, wants, and desires only go so far. How can you truly love someone else if you simply love yourself more (by wanting our needs and wants and desires met before the other's)? This is another form of cheap entertainment. It is where relational *infobesity* hijacks community. It is when our *infobesity* sabotages relationships with God and with others—because we want to be entertained.

9. McCracken, *Wisdom Pyramid*, 90.

Now, there is much debate on how relationships can thrive in digital spaces. For instance, can biblical community thrive in digital spaces? Is it possible to experience personal transformation and serve the needs of others in digital spaces?

The debate of building biblical community online has been researched by smart and capable experts. People from different professions, from clergy to theologians to counselors, have important views on the topic.

I have even had moments of heated debate on these viewpoints. For some people, biblical community can be formed online. To their own experiences, they share their development of participating in deep community online. They have grown in their faith and relationships through online church communities. I would agree. In addition to this, there are people who prefer online relationships rather than developing offline relationships due to their context. In these cases, people have searched for online discipleship because of their restricted backgrounds. Others have experienced genuine and real relationships online. Still others, however, believe biblical community can only thrive in face-to-face relationships.

According to our research on *infobesity*, there is evidence biblical community can thrive online and offline. In our experiences, online contexts are designed to connect and inform us. Online forms of community, discipleship, and evangelism are meant to bring us together. It is a beautiful form of being Jesus. With this being said, on site contexts of community are just as important. Offline and on site community is designed to transform us to become more like Jesus. The answer to the debate of relationships and spiritual formation should include offline and online expressions. These platforms should be promoted intentionally, relationally, and in each church context accordingly.

To encourage you, our *infobesity* participants have recognized their increased vulnerability with others online. People share their pain, personal concerns, and needs on a screen where they would be more reserved to share face-to-face. In addition to this, those who would never participate in a physical church were able to connect in small groups, friendship hubs, and mid-sized facilitated conversations through online platforms. It is an amazing gift digital spaces have given to the church.

CHAPTER NINE: COMMUNITY IN AN INFOBESITY WORLD

On the same hand, our research indicates online community—even though people have found meaning and significance through online relationships—only goes so far. Online community is a great tool to connect you and me with each other. But, the church is designed to be a transformational community, and as practiced in the early church, that is realized through face-to-face relationships.

I am thankful for the rise of digital platforms as a technological answer to build community and leverage influence for the church; the results are convincing. As we continue to expand and be digitalized in society, intentionality in building meaningful and significant community is strongly needed.

In the city I live in, modern-day loneliness has steadily increased. The urban jungle has become gradually lonelier. People live in isolated high-rise towers. Digital professionals focus on their careers rather than key relationships. People put their work ahead of forming healthy relationships. People work online and stay inside their personal towers. Due to this, people are becoming more and more isolated (and it is not just the city I live in).

When I have conversations with young and old, from different backgrounds and ethnic groups, there is a reoccurring theme of people searching for meaningful relationships and yet not knowing how to be relational. In one situation, as I was relaunching relational small groups throughout the city, I had someone ask me to participate in one of our downtown groups. Her exact request to me was, "I am recently divorced. I am looking for a singles small group in my area. I need the group to be no more than fifteen minutes away from me. And I am deeply lonely. I am needing quality relationships in my life. Can you assist me?"

As I listened to her request, my pastoral heart broke for her. Her marriage was done. She felt desperately alone. Her relational brokenness was evident. She was spewing out her heart to me. She needed help. I wanted to offer her hope in her seemingly hopeless attempt to fill the relational loneliness she was experiencing.

As I continued to talk to this lady, it became clear her desire for community was based on her own needs, wants, and requests. It is a human response. I get it. Nevertheless, it seemed to me she didn't want to be a part of a meaningful biblical community but wanted her needs met. As I mentioned to her I unfortunately did not have a singles group for her in her area, but

I did have a few groups available, her angst in our conversation grew. The hopelessness increased.

I continued to explain to her our community groups are designed to be transformational in nature. Very few of our small groups were demographic or theme-based. Instead, our groups are intentional, to empower people to become more like Jesus. I gave her three fantastic options, but sadly she was not interested in any of them. Unfortunately, I never heard from her again.[10]

This is the key problem of the deeply hyper-individualistic culture we live in. Intentional communities, marriages, deep friendships, united families, and personal transformation do not thrive when we personalize community towards our own needs and wants.

Think of the various relationships you know of which have deteriorated, rusted out over time, and busted out because personalized wants or needs or truths were more important than building healthy relationships.

Friend, Jesus promises a better way.

The New Testament church is a great model for our modern-day world. The early church never exercised hyper-individualism. The New Testament community trumped individual rights and fostered biblical community by practicing the one another commandments of Jesus.

Think of the story of Ananias and Sapphira.

They made the church community about themselves. Their story was about being served rather than serving others. In Acts 5:1–11, the story of Ananias and Sapphira is an example to all of us. This couple made up a story about sacrificial giving which was not the truth. Ultimately, they wanted to be praised and applauded for their generosity; and yet, because of their selfishness, they lied about their unselfishness. Ultimately, it cost them their lives (Acts 5:1–11).

---

10. This experience for me isn't an isolated case. I have had dozens of requests for relational community groups and yet, the requests are more interested in connection rather than Christlike transformation. I absolutely understand and observe the deep needs of this lady. Her requests and needs are real. I do not minimize her request, just be wary of her outcomes. To be honest, I pray and think of her often. I pray God will reach her deepest needs of loneliness and isolationism in our *infobesity* world.

Selfishness destroys the closest relationships, even with God.

I wonder, can our stories be like the story of Ananias and Sapphire? I think they can be. Is it possible we allow the personalization of culture and hyper-individualism seep into our own transformation in our local churches?

If we are honest with ourselves, our own selfishness can lead us to follow a version of Jesus more about us rather than being more like Jesus. Perhaps we have allowed ourselves to follow a nationalistic Jesus or a politicized Jesus. Perhaps we have followed a religious Jesus or a personalized Jesus rather than the Jesus of Nazareth.

It seems, when we are truly honest with ourselves, the rise of digital spaces and places in our lives have accelerated the hyper-personalization of self. The symptoms of *infobesity* reveal their ugly face in the polarization of our world, deterioration of key relationships in our families and friends, even with Jesus himself, and the local churches we call home.

Think about it: the cyclical nature of social information simply causes us to accentuate our own self-expression or self-gratification rather than have true relationships in our lives. The notion of social media followers or friends or likes or comments becomes more important to us, in our minds and hearts, rather than honoring people as Jesus has honored us.

Too often we have made Jesus, and what he has brought to humanity, more about ourselves than himself. The Pharisees did this. His family even did this. In fact, his closest friends did too.

If we are honest with ourselves, we can too.

For example, modern day cancel culture is nothing new. Cancel culture has been around for centuries. In fact, the religious leaders canceled Jesus. The political leaders, at the time, canceled him too. But Jesus never canceled anyone.

I get the modern-day cancel culture. I appreciate the justice cancel culture desires to seek. Social media has proven to provide an avenue for average people to leverage digital platforms as an opportunity to bring individuals to justice. However, cancel culture is limited too. How can we have justice without the option of mercy (a change of heart)?

PART TWO: RESPONDING TO INFOBESITY AS FOLLOWERS OF JESUS

Consider Jesus. He canceled cancel culture for good.

He exercised justice by canceling out the sins of the world. He took on the wrongdoings of broken humanity. He replaced the guilt and shame of sin with grace and truth. He carried the failures and limitations of human achievements with his mercy so you and I can have meaningful relationships with God and others.

Consider the woman caught in adultery (John 8:1–11). The gospel writer paints a picture of an angry mob going after this poor woman. Throughout the book of John, he presents the mob as a judgmental and hateful group of people. More than likely, the mob was stirred up by the religious leaders to cancel Jesus in lieu of the woman.

The mob never worked.

In this story, the mob wanted to cancel a woman caught in the most intimate way. Ripped out of the act and dragged to the center of the town where Jesus was visiting. This woman would have been humiliated in front of the whole town. Her guilt and shame center stage for everyone to see. It would be the equivalent of every intimate detail of your life being put online. How embarrassing! How humiliating! How hurtful! Everyone in the town would have watched this cancel story unfold on center stage.

Of course, according to John, the stage was designed to trap Jesus. The mob waited behind the scenes for their prey to take the bait and bring her to Jesus. They dragged her in front of Jesus. Jesus, at the time, was certainly teaching and ministering to people in the town. I imagine the mob interrupted the healing work of Jesus just to get justice. They would have demanded he do something about what this woman has caused.

How ironic.

The mob interrupted Jesus' healing work to get what they wanted from Jesus. John records Jesus wrote in the sand and said to the angry mob, "He who is without sin can cast the first stone" (John 8:7). And the Bible indicates one by one the mob dropped their stones and walked away, until it was only Jesus left with this woman in the center of town. We don't know who this woman was by name, but we do see Jesus compassionately redeeming her and not canceling her out. He graciously redeems her by saying to her, "Go and sin no more" (John 8:11b).

What an amazing story!

Jesus, who had no sin, had all the right to cancel this lady. He had the right to throw stones of shame, guilt, and condemnation at her. But he didn't. He restored her. He empowered her to have right relationship with God and with others.

Cancel culture does not do this. Modern-day cancel culture does not redeem. Forms of online cancelling are not biblical. Cancel culture is judgmental. Jesus does not judge us. He redeems us. He knows the most intimate details about you and me. He knows the dirt. He knows we should be canceled, but he doesn't do that. He shows compassion. He redeems. He restores.

We should do the same. Especially in digital spaces.

Too often, we do not practice the one another commandments of Jesus online. We cancel. We combat. We hurt each other. We troll. We criticize. We judge.

As followers of Jesus, this is not the way to be like Jesus online. I find it interesting the early church writers did not say, "Follow Jesus for yourself." They followed the "one another" commandments of Jesus with each other. Jesus challenged his earliest followers in the upper room, his closest disciples: "A new command I give to you: love one another" (John 13:34). Notice Jesus did not say "outsmart one another," or "blame one another," or "cancel one another," or "judge one another." No. He called his followers to love one another. A *new* command. A *new* way to live. A new SHEMA (שְׁמַע) (Deut 6:4).[11]

Imagine, the ancient Israelites experienced the mightiest acts of God when they were freed from their slavery in Egypt. For four hundred years representing twenty generations, the people of God were slaves to the Egyptians before God's miraculous activity.

Their identity, as a people, was based on human oppression. The heavy burdens of the Egyptian taskmasters made them feel like slaves. Their outlook on life was a life of slavery. The experience of Egyptian slavery developed

---

11. "To hear," meaning a new way of living is to be heard, listened, and acted upon.

a culture of slavery. Their identity as slaves should not go unnoticed by the readers of the Exodus narrative.

Think about it for a second. Let's put ourselves in the Exodus narrative. Maybe you can trace your family back for generations. For me, I can chart out three generations of my family. I am a fourth-generation Canadian, and my background is Ukrainian. My great-grandpa moved to Canada when he was only twelve. He traveled with his two older brothers, who were seventeen and nineteen at the time. Their parents could not afford the journey to Canada. They stayed in Ukraine for their children to have a better life in North America.

My great-grandpa's move to Canada had a difficult history. In between two World Wars, the three brothers settled in the prairies of Canada. To survive, my great-grandpa bootlegged alcohol during Prohibition and sold his liquor to the United States.

In comparison to modern-day times, my great-grandpa would be considered a drug dealer. He did this because there was no other way for him.

A generation later, my grandpa found himself experiencing Jesus at a schoolhouse church service. The history of his dad being a Canadian gangster changed the moment my grandpa gave his live to Jesus. My grandpa built a successful business. He worked hard as a rural farmer to provide a better opportunity for his family. The rest of my grandpa's story is forever changed.

My dad experienced Jesus as a boy too. His family raised him to know Jesus, work hard, be honest, and make the most of his life. He became a businessman of his own accord and worked hard to give us the life we have.

I am thankful for my history because it helps me understand my social identity. My family history reveals my values and heritage. I can stand on the shoulders of my family who went before me as they have shaped me into who I am today.

How about you? Can you trace your family history? Do you know how your family has uniquely shaped you, for good or for ill?

Now imagine, four-hundred years of history of Egyptian slavery for the people of God. Twenty generations of ancient tyranny. If I was an Israelite during that time, all I would know about myself, my history, and my identity would be slavery. It would be extremely difficult to see myself in any other way.

This is why God gave the ancient SHEMA from Moses in the book of Deuteronomy. He was calling them to live differently. Not as Egyptian slaves but as freed people. In God's eyes, the people of God were slaves no more.

Just like you and me. We are not designed to be slaves to modern-day digital addictions. We are meant to be children of God. Free to make the most out of our lives with Jesus. This is why the ancient SHEMA with the Israelites was more than a command. It was to be learned and practiced and memorized, to shape them after being freed from slavery. The SHEMA was to be exercised in relationship with God. It was through the SHEMA in the Pentateuch—the first five books of the Bible—that the Israelites re-identified themselves.

This is the same with you and me. Jesus is the new SHEMA empowering us to not be slaves to the digital trinity or to *infobesity*, but experience the divine purposes of a relationship with God.

In addition to the SHEMA of old, the episode on Mount Sinai took place to build a new identity for God's people. The promised covenant for the people of God was to experience the covenant with God as freed people. It was the opportunity for God's people to experience the full measure of freedom and relationship with God and each other as newfound children of God.

This reality is the same for you and me. We can experience the full measure of God in relationship with himself and with others. We get to experience the full SHEMA of God.

But there was another reason for God to provide the SHEMA to ancient Israel. It was to reveal a loving and everlasting God to the world around them. This concept of having a right relationship with God was to lead them to have the right relationship with other nations (and the world). This reality is important to understand.

Followers of Jesus, in old times and new times, and in digital times, God is clearly manifested by how followers of Jesus love one another. In fact, as Jesus quotes the SHEMA of old, he connects the SHEMA to you and me.

You might be asking yourself, "Well, how can I love people well? How can I practice one the another commandments of Jesus in our hyper-individualistic world?"

Skillfully; we do not need to love others on our own power or performance. We love others because Jesus has loved us first. Jesus is the way to pure love.

The concept of love sounds so shallow in our modern-day world, doesn't it? For instance, I can love my toothbrush, my coffee, my shoes, and my spouse all with the same word. The English translation of love is quite lame, to be honest. When it comes to the concept of love, modern-day society loves the idea of love but does not really know how to love.

Just listen to the Top-Forty hits.

The latest songs sing about love, but they are really singing about heartbreak. Artists sing more about the pain of love than truly loving others. Or consider the latest love songs. Artists sing songs about cheap love or bad love because bad love is better than no love. No one wants to be lonely! So, we offer cheap forms of love because no love leads to misery and modern-day loneliness. In all sincerity, if you listen closely to modern-day music, it is a cry for a better type of love.

Jesus showed a better type to love.

Jesus' love has purpose. His love leads to meaning and significance. His love leads to healthy relationships with family, friends, a spouse, or a potential spouse. The love of Jesus is a love this world cannot give (yet sings about). His love is meant to heal and restore. His love leads to Truth.

For me, one of the many benefits of God's purposeful love is that his love fills us. In the unlovable gaps in our lives, Jesus heals and restores us. He sets us free from the slavery of sin and mends us as children of God.

As Jesus is the same yesterday, today, and forever (Heb 13:8), we can invite his love in our pasts to heal us, to renew our present, and give us hope for our future. It is his love which restores the brokenness of our pasts, gives us courage for the present (by living and acting in his love), and to experience a preferred future in him. We can trust God's healing love because his love leads us to divine purpose for our lives.

But not only is his love purposeful, his love is practical. This is where the early church exercised the one another commandments of Jesus. Because of Jesus' love, we can experience right relationship with others. When his love heals and restores us personally, he empowers us to love others, to heal others, and to reveal Jesus in community. This includes our digital spaces. The old saying "hurt people hurt people" is true; but it is also true that "healed people heal people."

This is the work of Jesus being SHEMA.

The ultimate purpose of the one another commandments is to partner with God and his divine purpose to offer practical love to others who need divine healing.

We see it all around us. At school, at work, at our soccer games, in our churches, people need healing. Even in digital spaces, we have the opportunity to practically reveal God's love to others.

But not only is God's love purposeful or practical, his love is unconditional. In other words, there is no end to his love. There are no limits to his love.

So often, our world loves the idea of love but does not know how to truly love. The world screams of self-love or expressions of love or acts of love or personalizes love rather than truly experiencing love.

This is why the world needs Jesus.

He is the ultimate example of love.

In fact, he *is* love! (1 John 4:16)

Love is not love.

Love is God.

Jesus defines love, he exemplifies love, he is love, and he becomes the focal point of how to love others well.

Practically speaking, we can exemplify the love of God in our marriages, our families, with our friends, in our churches, and when we are online. When we love others well, the opportunities to reveal Jesus to our individualistic and broken world surge.

PART TWO: RESPONDING TO INFOBESITY AS FOLLOWERS OF JESUS

So, this begs the question: as followers of Jesus, how do we practice the one another commandments of Jesus in a hyper-individualistic and personalized world?

How do we build meaningful friendships, combat modern-day *infobesity*, and reveal the love of Jesus in a self-love world?

First, we need to know how to build authentic friendships. Aristotle, an ancient famous philosopher, identifies three types of friendships a person needs. We need these friendships to thrive in our world. He suggests (1) utility friendships, (2) hobby friendships, and (3) virtuous friendships.[12]

Utility friendships represent our workmates and classmates. For Aristotle, these types of friendships, known as acquaintances or social friendships, orbit approximately one hundred people in our lives. These people could include our neighbors or colleagues at work or friends on our sports team. These friendships bring joy around work or school. They are people who you mingle with and have helped you grow to become a better person.

For me, these types of friendships have included key teachers, teammates, and coaches throughout my life. I remember one of my teachers who intentionally spent more time with me. He spurred me on to be better with my educational goals. He would review my grades with me and encourage me to give my best in an upcoming exam. He practically showed me how to study (as I hated to study). He challenged my middle-adolescent bad attitude. Upon reflection, I realize he believed in me when I didn't. I am deeply thankful for his friendship.

His friendship, as a form of mentorship, changed my life! His investment in my life made me better. He cared enough to see me succeed. He shaped my life.

Another example of key utility friendships in my life was my high school basketball teams. In those teams, my coaches taught me how to be a better player. I learned how to be disciplined. I learned the benefits of hard work and the meaning of practice. I experienced the joys of celebrating wins with my teammates. I learned how to follow well.

---

12. Detweiler, *iGods*, 148–49.

CHAPTER NINE: COMMUNITY IN AN INFOBESITY WORLD

My coaches taught us how to serve each other on the basketball court. I learned how to bring out the best in other players. In reflection, these lessons followed me in my life. I am a better pastor, spouse, and father because of the lessons I learned with and from my sports friends.

For example, the values of teamwork, bringing out the best in others, and winning as a team have been foundational in my ministerial journey.

In your life, who have been the utility friends been in your journey? How have your workmates and schoolmates been there for you in your life? How have they shaped you to be better?

Aristotle does not just realize the importance of utility friendships; he also continues to share the significance of what he calls hobby friendships. Hobby friendships are people we like to have fun with. This could include a shared sport, activity, event, group, interest, or ministry where friendships are built.

For Aristotle, these types of friendships represent between twenty to fifty people in our lives at any given time. As Aristotle noticed, these relationships build strong social interactions with each other. In modern-day times, neuroscientists have realized strong friendships release stable serotonin levels to our brains. This allows us to experience joy, emotional strength, and lift our personal well-being simply by having a hobby we share with other people.

As each of us should have hobby-like friendships, Aristotle advocates for you and me to have these types of relationships in our lives. Aristotle perceived personal well-being was closely linked to the relationships we have. It is in these friendships, where we learn to laugh with, share an activity or interest with, express our burdens with, and ultimately to be able to be ourselves with others.

In New Testament times, hobby-based relationships represented the watering wells of society. These places were where people would gather to build friendships, connect about the day, and socialize with each other. One hundred years ago, the same mode of social relationships was practiced on front porches. It was at these places that people would process their day with each other.

However, in our modern-day context, people gather around digital spaces. As much as digital spaces are an opportunity for you and me to connect with one another, the ability to develop hobbies or activities is limited by screens. We need to be increasingly intentional in building hobby friendships with each other as we become digitalized as a society.

For me, I have found hobby friends at the gym. Over time, I have built meaningful community with my gym buddies. There have been times of encouragement, prayer, and spurring one another on. It is one of the watering wells in my life.

How about you, friend? Where are the watering wells where you can develop hobby friends? Who do you laugh with? Who do you shoot the breeze with? Who are the people in your life who bring life to you?

I think Aristotle is right that we need these types of people in our lives to thrive. In a world of *infobesity*, friendships are needed to combat the hyper-individualism and personalization fueled by digital spaces. Friendships call us out. Friendships keep us grounded. Friendships sharpen us to be better, not distracted by modern digital entertainment. Friendships invite us to a deeper meaning in our lives.

The last type of friendship Aristotle recommends is the most important type of friendship for our lives. He considers these friendships virtuous or character-based friendships. I would call them transformational relationships. These relationships help develop character in our lives.

According to Aristotle, virtuous friendships range between one to three people. It is these people who are close enough in our lives to be a transformative friend. These people could represent a family member, a coach, a teacher, a pastor, a youth leader, a mentor, a spouse, and can even be a small group of key friends. These types of friendships, as Aristotle highlights, are based on mutual love and respect. It is the friend you can call in the middle of the night. It is the one who, when you are in need, you text for prayer or encouragement or to walk with each other. It is the one who knows your deepest needs, insecurities, and brokenness and yet still want to be your friend.

This is the most coveted of friendships.

It is in these relationships where friends are practicing the one another commandments of Jesus with each other. This is where people not only thrive in life but are transformed to be more like Jesus.

In the context of our digital world, transformational friendships thrive best face-to-face. They develop the ability to be cognitively aware enough to understand nonverbal cues, sharpen relational skills, and develop social well-being. These types of relationships are linked to personal well-being including self-awareness, individual confidence, and productivity. As we see in the early church, it is in the face-to-face interactions where the one another commandments of Jesus are practiced well.

Not all of us are lucky enough to have transformational relationships in our lives. A modern-day professional counselor, Jonathan Haidt, has discovered people who do not have covenantal relationships are extra susceptible to high forms *infobesity*. Due to digital activity, people are either too isolated to exercise transformational friendships or they do not know how to thrive in transformational relationships. And unfortunately, digital spaces limit virtuous relationships.

Due to this, digital practices are a form of friendships (such as utility or hobby-based friendships) but limit transformational relationships in digital spaces.[13]

After a speaking engagement on *infobesity*, I had a young adult woman reach out to me online. She told me she created a technological "Way of Life" and built healthy digital habits in her personal life. She mentioned how beneficial the redemptive practices were to her. Her well-being increased as she combatted the *infobesity* she was experiencing. And yet, she acknowledged the damage effects of modern-day *infobesity* within her family. She admitted, "I am deeply lonely when I am with my family. At the dinner table we don't talk to each other. We do not interact with one another. We are on our phones when we eat."

She continued, "My parents don't ask me about my day. I feel like they don't want to be with me. What should I do?"

I applaud her for her digital self-awareness. She had the courage to challenge her digital addictions. She practiced digital habits to be redemptive

---

13. Detweiler, *iGods*, 152.

and purposeful. I am also sad for her family. Think about it. A young adult spotting the isolationism of digital practices at her own dinner table. She was reaching out for help. I coached her on a few social skills at the dinner table and asked her to keep me updated.

Her story is not an isolated case. I have had families connect with me to help them re-engage with each other because of the damaging effects they have experienced from *infobesity*. When it comes to transformational relationships, the ability to have one to three really close friends in our lives helps us battle with modern forms of digital addiction.

When you think about it, who are the transformational relationships in your life? Who is your mentor or significant other? Who is speaking into your life?

These friends are precious!

You might be asking yourself, "Well, how do I find these types of friendships in my life? Who are those transformational relationships for me?" Believe it or not, God has designed the local church for transformational friendships to thrive.

You can find all three circles of friendships of casual, hobby-based, and transformation friendships in a healthy local church, or as I call them, covenantal communities.

According to the research by the Evangelical Fellowship of Canada, meaningful and transformational friendships are practiced with no more than seven people. This is known as a covenantal community.[14] It is where your voice can be heard. It is where your name can be remembered. It is where people know who you are. It is where people ask how you are doing and listen.

In relational sciences, covenantal community is where meaningful relationships are built by practicing the one another commandments. When covenantal communities are limited to seven people, we see the quality of relationships increase. There is no competition to be had. People can

---

14. In monthly conversations with Rick Hiemstra, the quantitative study of the action research model, stakeholder on *infobesity*, and director of research and media relations for the Evangelical Fellowship of Canada (2020–present). See https://www.evangelical-fellowship.ca/Resources/Speakers/EFC-Speakers/Rick-Hiemstra.

intently share with each other, actively listen to each other, add meaningful dialogue to the discussion, and develop healthy relationships without social comparison.

It is a beautiful practice.

Online, it is difficult for covenantal communities to thrive. As individualism is the ultimate idol of our culture, people are continuously seeking, searching, and unfortunately, not finding meaningful community online. Yes, you can connect online. Yes, you may find friendships online. Yet this is not the context for transformational friendships to thrive; friendships thrive best in person.

As Aristotle has pointed out, we need all three types of friendships to flourish. It takes intentionality and self-awareness to practice the one another commandments of Jesus.

As a result of the lack of transformational friendships in our lives, it becomes easy to default to the culture of *infobesity*. We feed our own self-indulgences in relationships. We either compete for relationships or compare ourselves with those online.

This is not how God has designed community.

As followers of Jesus, we have the great opportunity amid a selfie-based culture to participate in transformational friendships. It is an amazing reality when we get to experience meaningful friendships through the one another commandments of Jesus.

To highlight a few, one another commandments we find in Scripture, we can implement these commandments when we are online.

The first one I want to highlight is how to honor one another. Paul, an early church leader, who wrote almost half of the New Testament, speaks of the concept of honoring one another as followers of Jesus. In Romans 12:10, he says, "Honor one another above yourselves." In this context, he is writing to the early church in Rome to consider each other of high value.[15]

In comparison, it would be like hosting a person of high stature in your home. Think of someone who you look up to or a famous person you'd like

---

15. Arndt et al., *Greek-English Lexicon*, 1005.

to meet. Imagine them wanting to come to your home to spend time with you. You would be honored to have them in your presence! It is in this same manner Paul is encouraging the early church to see each other. With high value and high regard.

In digital spaces, we do not necessarily know how to honor each other well. We do not view one another as of high value or high esteem. We tend to shout out our own information. We want to be validated before we validate others. We do not show honor and respect to others until we first experience honor and respect.

Jesus did not live this way.

He honored people. He loved people. He never disrespected or bullied people.

We should do the same.

For me, to honor people is an invitation by Jesus to reveal Jesus. I do this by not engaging in hateful or hurtful information. I steer online conversations over a coffee or to a one-on-one hangout rather than debating a topic for all the digital world to see. For me, I will not engage in certain topics. I will not engage in divisive situations. I do this because I want to represent people well online. It is an opportunity to practice the one another commandments of Jesus.

How about you? How can you honor people online?

As Paul continues in Romans 12:16, he encourages the Roman readers to "live in harmony with one another."

This means to have the same heart and mind as other people.

As we know, the online world can be a place of polarized views and opinions. It has caused deep relational hurts and pain rather than dialogue and understanding.

Paul realized this was happening in the Roman world as well. There were levels of social and intellectual classes, polarized views and opinions, and hyper-individualistic selfishness. Practically speaking, the reason people did not live in harmony with one another is because of their own prestigious pride.

Pride goes against the one another commandments of Jesus. In response, Paul is challenging the Roman Christians to live a better way. To live in harmony with one another.

We are challenged to do the same.

Imagine with me. What would it look like if Christians lived in harmony with one another online? What a difference it would make! To live in harmony with one another is to be able to understand and sympathize with one another.

In digital spaces, it is the invitation to see digital users not as economic units or content consumers but as human beings through the lens of Jesus. When someone comments negatively or criticizes us online, it is an invitation to understand and sympathize. Even when we are trolled by others, we get the opportunity to honor. It is a moment to create dialogue.

I have received countless negative comments online. I have had people criticize my content. I have had people misunderstand me. There have been many times people would not engage in dialogue. But that is OK.

Jesus was misunderstood. Jesus tried to engage people in dialogue and walked away. It is an opportunity to be like Jesus online.

In fact, if you go to my social media platforms, you can find some of these comments. For me, though, it is an opportunity to understand and sympathize with others. I respond, not react, with "tell me more," or "help me understand your perspective," or "that is interesting to say, please tell me more." There are times when people don't want to engage with me. It is OK. I simply say, "Thank you," and, "God bless you."

You see, our online activity is an opportunity to practice Christian love, honor, and respect. It is an invitation to love, honor, and respect (even when we do not deserve it, or others do not deserve it).

It is practicing SHEMA to a world far from God.

How can you practice SHEMA online? How can you show sympathy and respect to others?

Paul continues to inspire the Roman church. He carries on with them about the importance of the one another commandments of Jesus. In Romans

14:13 and 14:19, he encourages the early church "not to pass judgment on one another any longer," and to "pursue what makes for peace and for mutual upbuilding."

Paul is writing these words in the context of people literally stumbling over each other. The church in Rome was stumbling over relational tension and personal judgments. The early followers of Jesus were nitpicking each other. They were judging each other on what to eat, how to dress, and how to act. They would pick on each other about petty things.

They would class people into categories based on if they were poor or rich or young and famous. Due to this, people did not feel included in the church community. Paul is saying, "This is not good, friends!" We are meant to "live in peace with each other" to show Jesus to each other.

In the same way, we can use our digital spaces for peace, not judgment. Again, imagine the witness we could have if we were able to live in peace with one another. Imagine the online culture followers of Jesus could have if we did not stumble over one another in hurt and pain, but encouragement and love.

I try to follow this one another commandment by asking good questions. Rather than engage in harmful content online (even shared on my social media platforms), I ask good questions over content. This way, I am inviting people to dialogue, not debate.

If I am sharing content online, it is an opportunity to engage in relationships rather than judgments if I ask open-ended questions. I'd encourage you to do the same.

How can you engage in relationships over information online? I think it is possible. It is possible to point people to Jesus, who has the ultimate authority in our lives, rather than our own petty opinions and fleeting thoughts.

To tell you the truth, the one another commandments of Jesus have transformed my digital practices. I can see people online as people, not economic units. I can see digital users not as bits of information but as Jesus sees them. As a result, I have been able to intentionally engage with people online in healthy ways. I have revealed Jesus without pushing Jesus or sharing a judging Jesus. I have simply been Jesus. Not in political ways or polarized ways but by sharing hope, purpose, and healing through interaction, dialogue, and good questions.

Even my engagement strategy has changed online. I want to be redemptive with my digital habits and practices. Instead of the digital world clawing for my attention and to shape me in their images, I can shape the digital world to be a better place by being in his image.

I think this is what the online world is looking for. Content, relationships, community that points to the redemptive works of Jesus. I encourage you to practice the ninety-seven one another commandments of Jesus online. I challenge you to look at people not as digital consumers but opportunities to reveal Jesus in redemptive ways.

For the rest of our time together, we will be journeying through how to redeem digital spaces as followers of Jesus.

Personal Reflections

- Aristotle outlines three types of friendships human beings need to thrive. Which one do you need in your life?
- Who are the transformational friends walking with you in life? If you do not have one, how could you engage in a local church to find one?
- How can you start practicing the "one another" commandments of Jesus online?

PART THREE: Redeeming Digital Spaces

CHAPTER TEN: The Digital Practices of Jesus

> "God didn't go to all the trouble of sending his Son merely to point an accusing finger, telling the world how bad it was. He came to help, to put the world right again."
> —JOHN 3:17 (PETERSON, *Message*)

> "Jesus redeems everything."
> —APOSTLE PAUL (ROM 8:20–22)

Everything Jesus did was a response to the human heart. His words, his actions, his miracles were all about meeting, challenging, encouraging, and healing the human heart.

To Jesus, the human heart is the center of the human experience. This is why Jesus came to earth.

He engaged with all types of different hearts. He intrigued the religious. He invited the sinners. He interacted with the searching. He answered the skeptics. He was able to converse with every type of person because he desired to meet every human need of the heart.

Everything Jesus did was a response to you and me.

In a world bombarded by Instagram stories, short stories, and fleeting entertainment, the story of all stories is really Jesus.

PART THREE: REDEEMING DIGITAL SPACES

In a digital world bombarded by misinformation, disinformation, nonstop efficiency, and online connection, Jesus is the best story to share in digital spaces.

So often, rather than sharing the best story of Jesus, we share our own stories instead. Rather than building a Jesus brand online, we are more interested in building our own brands. There is no problem with building our own digital platforms and brands for education and work purposes, but when it comes to our personalized, hypersensitive, individualistic culture, we need to reflect on why.

As any storyteller would know, the best story wins. If we believe Jesus is the Story of *all* stories, then sharing his story of how he changed our stories can be the best engagement strategy online. So often, the entertainment loops online are consumer based; meaning, stories need to become increasingly entertaining for digital users to consume them. This is where, even as followers of Jesus, we are tempted to compromise our value systems to attract people to our digital places. It is a never-ending exhausting digital trap. Digital users and content creators have confessed to the pressures of online entertainment causing symptoms of *infobesity*. Decreasing personal well-being and compromising relationships. Digital content creators know what I am talking about.

As we have discovered in the pages of this book, it is Jesus who helps you and me to redeem our digital spaces. Not ourselves. When we invite Jesus into our digital practices, we are empowered by Jesus to build a digital brand that goes beyond ourselves.

How can we do this well?

Well, it starts with the practices of Jesus.

In the life and rhythms of Jesus, he regularly disconnected from the crowds to reconnect with God. In fact, the Gospels of Matthew (14:23), Mark (1:35), and Luke (5:16) all record Jesus consistently withdrew for prayer. Jesus retreated from the crowds. He removed himself from the popularity. He pushed back from the pressures of ministry life. He backed out of the entertainment loops to focus on his well-being. He connected with the Father. He realigned himself with purpose.

CHAPTER TEN: THE DIGITAL PRACTICES OF JESUS

Honestly, it is so easy to be entertained by crowds; especially online. It is terribly difficult to stay focused on what matters most when we are distracted by entertainment. When you and me have a video go viral or when the praise comments come in or new followers engage us, it is easy to be distracted by digital popularity. Unchecked, digital popularity can morph our sense of purpose. We can be become absorbed with the digital rather than the divine. We become formed into the image of the digital trinity rather than the Holy Trinity. Yet, we see Jesus never caved in to the crowds because of his popularity. He stayed focused on his purpose.

In his book *Deep Work: Rules for Focused Success in a Distracted World*, Cal Newport shares how our brains are wired to become easily distracted.[1]

The numerous online notifications, email alerts, and digital dings are designed to distract you and me from deep focus. It is in times of deep work where our most creative thoughts are developed. Depending on your daily rhythms, our most creative and productive work is when we are not distracted. It means our brains are relaxed. Our emotions are steady. We are not stressed out or burnt out from anxiety. Our surroundings are quiet and calm. Our well-being is centered.

This is what Jesus exemplified when he went away to quiet places.

For me, I am most focused in the mornings. My brain is relaxed. I feel fresh and my creative thinking kicks into high gear. During these times, I block it off for creative thinking or writing or projects. I take time to reconnect with God as it aligns me to deep, productive, and inspired work.

I turn off the digital alerts. I go to a quiet place. I allow my creative thoughts to flow. I write down what I feel God is sharing with me, and allow him to work through me in my creative process.

This only happens when I am centered with Jesus.

When we are focused, not only are we creative or productive, but we are relaxed. We are centered. I don't know about you, but my daily life can become hectic. It is important for me to slow down enough to hear from God for the day before the day starts. When I was single, I would center

---

1. Newport, *Deep Work*, loc. 51, Kindle.

myself with God whenever I wanted. My time was flexible and fluid. I could disconnect from the world to reconnect with God anytime I wanted.

However, living in a world constantly connected to digital spaces, we need to become increasingly intentional in disconnecting from the digital to reconnect with the divine.

With all the digital noises, voices, and bombardment of cheap entertainment, it is too easy to be distracted, confused, and frustrated with the realities of life. Even in my own life, when I do not disconnect to reconnect with God, my *infobesity* symptoms want to rise.

The Gospel writers noticed how Jesus "often withdrew to lonely places and prayed" (Luke 5:16 NIV). He went to be in "lonely places" (NIV), the "wilderness" (NLT, NASB), or to the "desolate" (ESV) to pray! For Jesus, these places would have included being outdoors and in creation.[2] He simply retracted himself from the busyness of life to slow down to be with the One who is the maker of life.

Where do you go to find quiet places?

How do you slow down enough from the busyness of life and the modern-day distractions of digital spaces to reconnect with Jesus?

When I reflect on these questions, whether I am stuck in traffic or waiting for the hockey game to start, I innately want to pick up my digital device. I want to scroll through my social media feeds, check my texts from friends or family, and follow up on my business emails. I have even found myself wanting to engage with my digital device when I am in my quiet space waiting to hear from God. So often, I instinctively pick up my digital device when I should be connecting with the divine.

Can you resonate with me?

I think we have been too distracted when we have tried to reconnect with God.

We are too easily distracted, constantly, with the flashy realities of the digital world wanting to drown out the voice of God in our lives. It is amazing to me that Jesus is gracious enough to speak to us when we reconnect with

---

2. Elwell, *Baker Encyclopedia of the Bible*, 2:2141 (s.v. "wilderness").

him. He does not phubb us. He does not reject us. He simply waits for us. What a great reality we have as followers of Jesus.

Despite this, we need to build space and time to be with Jesus. Just like Jesus did to reconnect with his Father, we need to do the same. When we hear from God in quiet places, he refreshes us in purpose, healing, and life.

Not only did Jesus retreat to quiet places, he built rhythms of rest. In the context of the Gospel writers, Jesus would pray to "speak to or to make requests to God"[3]—to find rest in God.

Jesus would rise early in the morning or late at night. Scriptures indicate Jesus brought his concerns, cares, frustrations, feelings, thoughts, questions, and struggles to God in prayer. He would be honest, sincere, real, and raw. He didn't need to default to the culture around him to find answers. He went to God; especially when he needed courage and strength. In fact, Jesus' example paved the way for you and me to have these types of prayers with God too. We can be real with God. We can be raw with our requests. We can be honest with God knowing he hears our prayers. He is not scared by our prayers. He isn't shocked with what we ask. We can confidently come to God in prayer, as he provides rest and right perspective.

Because Jesus took on the sins of the world, we, too, can come to God in boldness—meaning, we do not need to be scared of God. God wants you and me to know him, to hear from him, and to respond to our prayers.

Now, let's pause here for a second. You might be asking yourself, "Really, Andy? God answers my prayers? Yeah, right! I have not experienced God answering my prayers in a long time." But it is true.

He does answer our prayers! All the time.

We might not like his answers to our prayers but we can trust his response. He knows us—better than ourselves!

He knows what's best for us even before we know what's best for us. He knows us because he loves us. He created us. So, yes, approach God with all confidence; God is waiting to speak to us.

---

3. Louw and Nida, *Greek-English Lexicon*, 1:408.

For me, connecting with God is more than getting an answer. For me, spending time with Jesus is getting to know Jesus. Prayer is deeper than being real with God. The other side of prayer is listening to God. To apply what he is saying to you and to me. This is the greatness of prayer. God speaks to us—personally, with all divine wisdom of his grace and truth to help us be more like Jesus in our digital world. Amazing reality, to be honest! In prayer, all of heaven is speaking to our hearts. To instill courage, insight, and right relationship with him.

Even in the difficult seasons of my life, listening to his voice has provided renewed strength. When I am exhausted or tired or frustrated, he supernaturally provides. His whispers give followers of Jesus the advantage to experience courage in our hearts and minds.

This is why we should practice a digital sabbath.

A digital sabbath allows you and me to experience the spiritual practice of rest. This means there is an intentional "period of time" set aside to reconnect with God. We see, in Genesis 1 and 2, God took a twenty-four-hour period to rest from his work (Gen 2:2–3). In the Gospels, we see Jesus declaring he is the new Sabbath, literally, inviting people to experience spiritual well-being to the weary, the confused, the shattered, and the weak (Matt 12:1–8; Mark 2:23–28; Luke 6:1–5). God designed the Sabbath for humanity to enjoy by reconnecting with God—to experience his presence, his peace, his joy, and his company in prayer as we live in a world of *infobesity*.

What great hope we have as followers of Jesus.

I would encourage you—disconnect from the digital. Take a digital sabbath to reconnect with the divine. Schedule a twenty-four-hour period away from digital spaces. Take a break from the pressures of always being online. Rest from work. Disconnect from digital entertainment. Disengage from the online information, and simply be with God. It will change your life for the better! In fact, it has changed mine when I have done this.

You see, we live in a world of digital addiction. The practices and prayer of Jesus in quiet places give you and me the ability to overcome digital addiction.

CHAPTER TEN: THE DIGITAL PRACTICES OF JESUS

Digital addiction is a relatively a new term. Since COVID, digital addiction has been readily present in people's lives. It is when digital users gravitate to online practices as a coping mechanism to deal with difficult realities in life.

As mentioned throughout the book, a symptom of *infobesity* is the addictive nature of digital spaces. This phenomenon of modern-day addiction can lead us to digital sins.

As we have seen through the pages of Scripture, sin can become addictive. Sin can be flashy. Sin feeds our human need to be entertained. Unfortunately, digital sins—like human sin—lead to overpromising and underdelivering. Addictive behavior, like sin, can consume us. Digital addiction can shape us according to our sinful patterns rather than living in purpose and meaning with Jesus.

This is why we should participle in a digital sabbath.

Overwhelmingly, participants in our *infobesity* self-assessment have responded to their digital practices and habits as addictive. These practices have included secret social media platforms, burner accounts, sexual content, inappropriate online relationships, and harmful communities. To these participants, engaging in digital sins have revealed their lack of discernment strategies in filtering through digital activity. They have not let the redemptive practices of Jesus into their online practices. Hence, becoming addicted to their digital practices.

Consequently, digital practices and habits become personalized. Just like sin, these practices isolate us from each other. We keep our digital habits in the dark. Rather than confess our digital sins to Jesus, we hide them. We create private accounts. In reaction, we do not want others to know what we are doing online. We keep Jesus distant. This is the dangerous cycle of digital sins controlling our lives.

Followers of Jesus overcoming digital addiction need to engage in redemptive practices. We need to confess digital sins. We need to keep our digital habits in the light. We need to invite Jesus into our platforms. We need to allow him to know about our digital activity.

In our research, participants who were able to overcome digital addiction and experience increased well-being implemented the redemptive practices from the *infobesity* self-assessment. They realized the harmful and damaging consequences of *infobesity*. Participants created new habits around their digital practices. They confessed their digital addictions.

One of the first disciples of Jesus brilliantly wrote about confession. He put it this way: "Confess your sins to God, who is faithful and just to forgive your sins and cleanse you from all unrighteousness" (1 John 1:9 NIV). This means we can confess our sins, including our digital sins, to God. He does not condemn us or shame us. He sets us free from digital sins in confession. Let me put it this way: Jesus invites you and me to bring our digital addiction to him.

When John wrote these words, he was expressing two realities. First, he is reminding his readers sin is real. Sin affects our well-being. Sin destroys purpose. Sin separates us from God. Sin deteriorates relationships around us. Including digital sins.

He is revealing the need to confess our sins as an attitude—as a behavioral position with God. We cannot micromanage sin or shift responsibility from sin—we need to confess sin. It is an attitude of choice.

Second, John is reminding his readers of the power of confession. When we act in confession, there is a supernatural promise. God forgives us. Through confession, we can experience freedom from shame and guilt. He cleanses us from digital sins. Confession invites Jesus into our digital activities and sets us on a journey to experience freedom from *infobesity*.

I want to encourage you today: if you are wrestling with digital sins, Jesus has provided a way to experience freedom from digital addiction. It is a simple digital practice through confession. It is a supernatural act. As we live in a digital world, confessing our digital sins is an important attitude to live by. As followers of Jesus in an infobese world, we can experience freedom from digital addiction. In addition to this, not only does Jesus forgive us, but he cleanses us. He offers practical steps to become whole. He points us to positive well-being.

You can develop a technological "Way of Life." You could start an *infobesity* small group in your youth ministry. You could participate in a local church. Why not build a covenantal community with your friends? Find a mentor who can help transform your digital practices to be redemptive. These are digital practices you and I can live by as followers of Jesus.

I find sin does weird things to us when we do not keep our lives in the light. Sin wants to keep us in the dark. Sin wants to keep our digital practices private. Sin, even though enticing and addictive, never leaves us better as people.

Sin destroys us.

When we are able to keep our sins in the light through prayer, Sabbath, and confession, then you and I will be able to experience freedom from digital addiction.

We will experience personal well-being. We will find wholeness and renewed purpose. We will experience digital freedom. With this reality, we can reveal Jesus in digital spaces.

Personal Reflections

- Out of the digital practices of Jesus (prayer, Sabbath, and confession), which one jumps out to you? Why?
- How will you practice a twenty-four-hour digital sabbath?
- Which digital sins do you need to confess to God today?

CHAPTER ELEVEN: Building a Jesus Brand for the Digital World to See

"Christianity worked at the grassroots level."
—Gerald L. Sittser[1]

"The Christians' lifestyle is rooted in hope. In contrast, impatience is hopeless."
—Alan Kreider[2]

Since the birth of the church in the book of Acts, the church has had a unique opportunity to reveal Jesus to the world. Historians—skeptics, atheists, and believers alike—have attributed the enormous amount of growth of Christianity to three realities.

First, the church thrived because of Christlike hospitality. The church during the height of the Roman Empire flourished because the early church engaged with people. They served people well as Jesus served people well. They practiced the one another commandments with all types of people in a culture based on elitism. They considered all people equal, unique, and purposeful. They loved one another. They ate with one another. They prayed for one another. They deeply cared for people. First-century Christians were a spiritual family.

The hospitality of the early Christians would have been foreign to the Roman Empire. The Romans only took care of themselves. Based on your

---

1. Sittser, *Resilient Faith*, 308.
2. Kreider, *Patient Ferment of the Early Church*, 23.

social status, you would be subjected to the status quo of the day. No one took care of those from a lower status. And yet, the church did. In fact, historians have traced modern-day hospitals and care facilities' roots back to the hospitality of Christians in the first three centuries of Christianity.

Second, the church thrived in the Roman world because of personal transformation. Followers of Jesus practiced their faith in everyday life. They followed Jesus even if it could have cost them. For some, being a follower of Jesus cost them their financial well-being. For others, followers of Jesus experienced family rejection. Even more so, first-century followers of Jesus paid with their lives.

This type of personal transformation in the early church was intentional. Followers of Jesus lived like Jesus. They lived in community—not to connect with acquaintances or hobby-like friends, but to build transformational communities. These communities became hubs of prayer, learning and teaching the Ways of Jesus, and practicing the commandments of Jesus throughout the Roman world.

As a matter of fact, the intentional learning communities of the early church created universities and colleges. Universities were a Christian idea.

As the early church would meet in homes and villas, followers of Jesus learned how to be like Jesus in a communal experience. They practiced a relational learning model. They walked with one another to be like Jesus in real life. Learning didn't just happen in a lecture hall but in relationships. Modern-day university campuses have brilliantly been inspired by the early church to adopt biblical modes of learning.

Unfortunately, the recent history of university thought has been a hotspot for modern-day hate and extremist learning. Rather than learning in relational dialogue with each other, extreme thought has been inspired. Rather than respect or honor being practiced, judgment and anger have polarized students, teachers, and society. We need to return to an early church model of learning from one another.

Third, the early church thrived in the secular, sexualized, and individualized culture of ancient Rome. Even with the onslaught of Christian persecution in the Coliseum, the church grew with influence.

Experts suggest two hundred thousand to four hundred thousand people died in the Roman Coliseum. Over one million exotic animals, in the span of four hundred years, would have been slaughtered in Rome alone. Starting in 100 AD, followers of Jesus were routinely martyred. Christians heroically saw such tyranny as an opportunity for the world to see Jesus.

It is historically known that the first Christian martyr in the Roman Coliseum was Bishop Ignatius of Antioch. His martyrdom was recorded in the late first century. According to his hagiography (it is historically verified), Ignatius believed his death in the Roman Coliseum was an opportunity to reveal Jesus to the world. He saw his death in the Coliseum as center stage for all to see.[3]

At the time, the Coliseum could hold up to eighty-five thousand people[4] and would represent all of Rome. The rich, the poor, the young, the old, the prestigious, the well-known, and the disenfranchised were all a part of the Coliseum games. At the peak of the Roman world, one million people lived in the city of Rome and the Coliseum was the center of Roman news, commerce, economics, social status, culture, and entertainment. Ignatius saw his death as a chance to reveal Jesus.

History indicates Ignatius—and many others like him—would praise God, hold hands, and quote Scripture before their deaths. They would pray for one another. They would help each other up if knocked down by gladiators or wild beasts. Eyewitnesses recorded they would recognize followers of Jesus' unique (and bizarre) disposition, as they did not fear death. This type of Christian behavior was noticed by the crowds. Their response to their imminent death was the opposite from the criminals and gladiators in the arena.

They were peaceful.

They seemed to have no fear.

They would worship God.

---

3. Schoedel, *Ignatius of Antioch*, 13.
4. This would include sitting- and standing-room only.

CHAPTER ELEVEN: BUILDING A JESUS BRAND FOR THE DIGITAL WORLD TO SEE

For followers of Jesus, the Coliseum was an opportunity for the world to see Jesus.[5]

Possibly, as we live in a digital world, followers of Jesus have a great opportunity to reveal Jesus for everyone to see.

Perhaps you and I can reveal Jesus to an anxious, fearful, depressed, broken world wrestling with *infobesity*. Perhaps we can reveal a better way.

Maybe, just maybe, we can share the Story of all stories rather than our own stories. Perhaps we can make Jesus famous rather than try to make ourselves famous.

This is the heart of our time together. How can you and I make Jesus famous in a digital world where everyone wants to be famous?

It is not unusual to meet students who want to be the next big thing online. They want to start up a YouTube channel in the hopes of going viral. Or to develop the next best social media platform. I have had countless conversations with university students wanting to design the next app to hit it big and get rich.

It seems younger generations are motivated to do whatever it takes to become rich and famous from digital platforms. Even as I am writing this, an eighteen-year-old young man decided to unbuckle his seat belt on a popular roller coaster. He lifted the handlebars to take an extreme TikTok reel from his perspective. Unfortunately, he was not able to record or post his video because the roller coaster flung him off of the ride. Consequently, he suffered serious injuries.[6] His phone was busted too . . .

Too often in our modern-day culture, we want to pursue what will make us famous. We share our own stories rather than share the Story of all stories. But, as we have seen throughout this book, digital space has over-promised and under-delivered. The human experience of online technologies has its limitations.

We are made for more. We are made to make Jesus known.

---

5. Little, "Five Ways Christianity Spread," para. 15.
6. See Freeman, "Video Shows Moment Paramedics Helped Victim."

In our digital spaces, how can you and I make Jesus known? How can we shift from building our own brands to developing a Jesus brand instead? Could we learn from the early church to find ways to make Jesus famous in a world where everyone wants to be famous?

To date, over five billion people are online each day. Five billion people (and growing)! Five billion people interact on social media. Five billion people engaging with online content. Five billion people consuming digital information. What a great opportunity we have as followers of Jesus.

We have the access, ability, and creativity to share the good news of Jesus with the world like never before. As we see through the Gospels, the life of Jesus reveals how he engaged with the world. His engagement strategy is a great example for you and me to engage with the world online. And it is this engagement strategy for you and me to inform people, interact with people, inspire people, and invite people into the story of Jesus.

Let's unpack how Jesus engaged with the world.

First, Jesus engaged with people through modes of information with his words. His words are the most famous words in the world. In fact, his discourse on the Sermon of the Mount were the greatest words of information ever recorded (Matt 5–7). It is in these famous words that Jesus informs humanity of a better way to live. He speaks about how to live as kingdom people living a kingdom-based life in a world of earthly kingdoms. He outlines what a kingdom person looks like. He informs the crowds about prayer, generosity, how to treat one another, forgiveness, practical love, and kingdom perspective. In the same way, Jesus informs you and I how to live a real faith in everyday life by being kingdom people.

As we have discovered throughout this book, information is the foundational level of engagement in digital spaces. As information is shared online, the basic forms of information is categorized to either social information, misinformation, disinformation, practical information, and/or harmful information. Online creators understand the styles of information where digital users can increase digital engagement. But, as followers of Jesus, the base form of information we can engage digital users with is called helpful information.

Helpful information is online content designed to help others. Helpful information can inform digital users of an event or a small group or a connecting point. It can be helpful information of an upcoming service or sermon or inspired quote from you or me. We can be a source of helpful information for those who are struggling.

When Jesus informed the crowd with the Sermon on the Mount, he was giving people helpful information. He was engaging people with information to live a better life. In the same way, we can use our own platforms and influence to help digital users to experience a better way to live in a world of *infobesity* through helpful information.

This is why we need to see Jesus as the divine Tekton. The power of the Spirit of Truth can lead us in creative ways to share helpful information online in the motivation to redeem information online.

As followers of Jesus, we may not get the highest engagement when we share helpful information online, but that is not the point. Our online engagement should point people to Jesus.

But not only did Jesus engage people with helpful information (which represents 10 percent of the information Jesus shared on earth), we see Jesus' engagement with the world was through forms of interactive information.

Thirty percent of everything Jesus said or did was a response to a question. In other words, Jesus dialogued with people. The science behind interactive information is the ability to expand conversations with each other. Think about it for a second: when someone asks you a question, for example, it is initiated by a person—whatever their intent and content—to engage with you in dialogue, collective wisdom, and ongoing conversation. When someone asks a question, they are eager to engage with the information you are interacting with.

Let me put it this way. When people ask questions, it is an invitation from them to enter a conversation. A deeper conversation. A conversation of safety, engagement, mutual respect, and enjoyment.

Jesus interacted with people using questions as a form of social engagement.

When we do not ask questions, it is because we do not feel safe to ask our questions. We think we will be embarrassed or ridiculed. We do not ask questions in our small groups or schools or at the dinner table, perhaps, because we fear what others will think. But Jesus created safe places to ask our questions and to answer our questions.

In our research, we recognized that those who did not have safe places or safe people to ask their questions about life, meaning, and purpose would go to digital spaces instead. They would go to Google first rather than God. There is nothing wrong with going to Google. But, as we do, those who are looking for answers do not necessarily get the right answers. It is a plethora of information rather than answers. Even with this being said, Google's answers to our questions are based on our own biases, preferences, and values rather than interacting with information towards truth.

People felt safe around Jesus. All types of people asked him their questions. His followers, skeptics, sinners, and haters asked him questions around authority, the kingdom, and clarity on his teachings. To Jesus, some of the questions asked of him were genuine. Other questions were asked in frustration. A few questions were meant to be sarcastic or hurtful. But, as we see, Jesus responded to peoples' questions with love and grace.

In the ministry years of Jesus, he was asked 307 questions, asked 183 questions himself, and answered 3 questions.[7] The 3 questions Jesus answered were a direct response to his authority.[8]

You see, Jesus interacted with people. He used dialogue and conversations rather than monologue and lectures to share information.

In the same way, as followers of Jesus living in a digital world, could we interact with people online? Could we dialogue and develop healthy forms of conversation for people to ask their questions about life, meaning, and purpose?

If we do, then our engagement strategy online will reveal Jesus.

In my digital practices, the most engagement I have experienced is when I ask open-ended questions. These questions have included, "How can I pray for you?," "If you could meet with Jesus, what would you want to say

---

7. Woolley, "Questions Jesus Asked," para. 8.
8. Smith, "Jesus Answers All His People's Questions," para. 6.

CHAPTER ELEVEN: BUILDING A JESUS BRAND FOR THE DIGITAL WORLD TO SEE

to Him?," and "I am speaking on _____, what would you want me to say?"

When I ask my questions online, I am inviting digital users to a conversation. I am encouraging people to engage in forms of interactive information.

As you may know, information has been flatlined in digital spaces. Anyone can find anything they want online. This is why conversational dialogue is so important in our world today.

And with the rise of artificial intelligence, forms of learning are changing. For example, though students are still studying information, teachers are asking for reflective or dialogical or collaborative approaches to learning to increase retention in students. Sharing information alone is not enough for learners to engage with it. It is extremely important to build retention with relational learning.

This is what Jesus did two thousand years ago.

When we ask good questions online, we are inviting people into an intentional conversation. We are engaging in relational learning. A collaborative approach to interacting with information.

When we ask good questions, we are not trapping people into a debate. We are not polarizing people. We are building relationships with one another, like Jesus did.

In all honesty, I have become a better pastor, teacher, preacher, and person by dialoguing with people online. When I ask good questions, I am inviting people to make me a better person.

At times, I have asked how to become a better speaker online. I have interacted in digital spaces with others, collaborating on how to equip young pastors. I have had great conversations with people when they feel safe in their thoughts, opinions, and suggestions.

I have prayed with strangers. I have interacted with skeptics of Jesus. I have counseled people who have experienced church hurt (which is real). I have stayed in touch with so many simply because I have tried to create safe places online.

How about you? How can you create safe places in your digital spaces?

In all honesty, I want to be known for creating safe places online. I want to be know as someone who is willing and able to have good conversations with open-ended questions, building relationships and sharing information about the Way of Jesus. I want to be known for interacting with people online, using that as an opportunity to engage with digital users and point them to Jesus. I think this is how Jesus would respond online. How about you?

Think about how Jesus has engaged you and me; he interacts with us, doesn't he? He whispers his answers to us in our prayerful questions. He reveals himself through Scripture, the stories of the Gospels, and through the Spirit of Truth, to our hearts and minds.

He invites you and me to trust him. Even when our questions are not answered, we are encouraged to trust him when he is silent.

In the same way, may I encourage you to engage with the online world like Jesus? How can you ask good open-ended questions? How can you invite digital users through purposeful questions where respect, dialogue, and ongoing conversations can thrive?[9]

Not only did Jesus develop an engagement strategy around helpful information and interactive information, but he also inspired people with information through stories.

When you read the stories Jesus shared, he was a master storyteller. To tell you the truth, Jesus shared stories more than any other form of information in his ministry. Sixty percent of Jesus' words were communicated through short stories known as parables.

Parables are distinct. Parables are forms of storytelling around an image or illustration or person. Jesus used stories, such as parables, to communicate a kingdom principle. Jesus used imagery so his hearers could understand. He shared stories, illustrations of sand, trees, animals, and the cosmos, for truth to be experienced. He pointed to exemplary people, like the good Samaritan, as an opportunity to prove a kingdom point. For Jesus, his stories were modes of information to inspire people to be kingdom people in everyday life.

---

9. Feel free to go to www.infobesity.ca for a list of open-ended questions to engage with digital users.

CHAPTER ELEVEN: BUILDING A JESUS BRAND FOR THE DIGITAL WORLD TO SEE

As Jesus inspired people through storytelling, we can do the same. We can share short stories online of how God is working in us. We can share stories of God working in and through us each and every day. In fact, modern-day sciences have determined the human brain is wired to remember stories better than any other form of information.

What a key strategy you and me can engage with online.

But not only was Jesus a master storyteller; we see members of the early church were master storytellers too. They shared stories about the kingdom of God in their lives. For example, in the New Testament, the early church would share stories known as testimonies.

Testimonies are stories of God's redemptive work in an individual. In the glorified Gospel of Jesus, known as Revelation, John encourages followers of Jesus to overcome the world "by the blood of the Lamb, and by the word of their testimony" (Rev 12:11).

In other words, John is saying the power to engage the world is to share our stories of how the Master Storyteller, Jesus, changed our stories. It is the art of sharing our testimonies of redemption, healing, and the ongoing work of Jesus in our lives for the world to see online.

When John wrote these words in Revelation 12:11, followers of Jesus were encountering Roman persecution. Christians were being thrown in jail, ripped from their families, having their wealth taken from them, and even having their lives taken. For John, sharing their testimonies with one another inspired them to live for Jesus amid the horrendous persecution they were experiencing.

In addition to this, John's words to the church in Revelation are how storytelling, through our testimonies, show how we can engage a secular world, hostile and skeptical of Jesus.

When we share our stories of personal transformation online, we reveal Jesus to the world. When we share our testimonies, we encourage other followers of Jesus to do the same.

I call this a Jesus brand.

PART THREE: REDEEMING DIGITAL SPACES

As followers of Jesus, we are called to build a Jesus brand online. We are not just about building our own brands but sharing stories of God's redemptive work in our lives. I believe this is an untapped opportunity for you and me online.

This doesn't mean you and I must share a lifelong testimony online. It means sharing a story of God working in our lives each and every day.

Could you? Would you share God's work in your life online?

For me, I encourage people to share stories on their personal struggles. It could be a mental health issue or how to find courage and strength during personal challenges. It could be a short story of hearing God or how he answered a prayer request.

However we share our stories online, the key is to share the love of Jesus. This means we share stories, helpful information, interactive information, and information to inspire one another to live a better life on this planet.

Like no other time in human history, followers of Jesus can engage billions of people through their digital platforms. We can inspire one another, encourage one another, and engage digital users in positive and redemptive ways.

You might be asking yourself, "How can I share good stories online?," or "How can I be a testimony in digital spaces?"

Well, a mentor of mine, Leonard Sweet, suggests EPIC storytelling. He puts it this way: EPIC storytelling is "an (E)xperience of God that is (I)mage rich, (P)articipatory, and (C)onnectional."[10] I think this is a great template of how to share stories online. Stories which include our everyday (e)xperiences, (p)ractical advice on how to encounter Jesus, using (i)mages and stories that (c)onnect people to Jesus.

Just like Jesus was a master storyteller, and like the early church sharing stories through personal testimonies, may you and I be inspired to share stories online. We can build a better brand. A Jesus brand. A brand to engage a world confused by *infobesity*.

---

10. Sweet, *Giving Blood*, 24 (brackets mine).

CHAPTER ELEVEN: BUILDING A JESUS BRAND FOR THE DIGITAL WORLD TO SEE

When we build a Jesus brand, we point people to the Story of all stories, Jesus. We do not point to our own stories or to our own brands alone. We don't engage in the digital trinity of cheap entertainment, unlimited consumption, and access. We do not create our own modern-day shiny idols. We point people to Jesus.

Could we do the same? Can we point people to Jesus in digital spaces? Can we be EPIC storytellers?

Jesus shared helpful information, interactive information, and inspired information through storytelling; he did this to inspire people to purpose. The famous words of Jesus, "I have come to bring life and life to the full" (John 10:10), is an invitation to all. He came to invite you and me to live life to the fullest. Not to be confused or conflicted or chaotic in a world ruled by *infobesity*. And yet, Jesus invites you and me to invite people to purpose too.

This is the invitation of Jesus. Truth be told, Jesus *is* the invitation.

He is the invitation to purpose, to meaning, and to significance. He is the invitation for the world to see as you and I build a Jesus brand online.

In the Gospels, Jesus invited a rich young ruler him to let go of his *infobesity* of stuff and follow a better way.[11] Jesus wasn't inviting the rich young ruler to forsake everything. He was inviting him to everything—found in Jesus. Jesus was inviting him to experience full life. For the rich young ruler—who, it could be argued, could represent you and me in our rich modern-day Western world—was to let Jesus be his everything rather than his pursuit for everything. At the end of the story, the rich young ruler's wealth was more important to him than living in purpose with Jesus.

Jesus invited the woman caught in adultery to live a new life of purpose. He offered her hope and a new beginning. He lifted the weight of shame and guilt in her life for her to live a better way of life (John 8:1–11). She accepted Jesus' invitation, experiencing redemption, purpose, and new life.

Jesus invited the woman who had five husbands into a new way of life. She was considered an outcast. She would be known as a liability. Still, Jesus invited her to a new way of thinking. And to live in a new standard of living

---

11. See Matthew 19:16–30; Mark 10:17–31; Luke 18:18–30.

(John 4:4–42). A kingdom standard. She accepted Jesus' new way of life; experiencing joy, personal renewal, and hope for her future.

Jesus invited the tax collector Zacchaeus to a higher way of living. Zacchaeus was invited by Jesus to spend time with him. At the end of the conversation between Jesus and Zacchaeus, Zacchaeus lived a life of generosity (Luke 19:1–10). He became a person offering meaning and purpose to those around him rather than living for himself in a life of greed and politicking.

Just like Jesus invited the rich young ruler or the woman caught in adultery, just like the woman with five husbands, and the greedy tax collector Zacchaeus, he invites you and me to a better way of life. He invites us to build a Jesus brand.

He invites us to reveal Jesus online. He invites you and me to redeem digital spaces.

In the digital world, the invitation by Jesus is for everyone. Everyone who wants to live a better way. What a great opportunity. Followers of Jesus can share Jesus' invitation to five billion people who are online each and every day.

Just like the early church in a secular, hypersexualized, and highly individualized culture in ancient Rome, followers of Jesus considered themselves honored to share their stories. They knew their lives were at stake if they built a Jesus brand. But for the early followers of Jesus, to reveal Jesus to the Roman world was an *epic* story. They literally practiced Revelation 12:11.

They didn't build their own brands. They built a Jesus brand. They didn't think of their own lives as to be saved, but to be served up as a sacrifice. In the same way, as we live in a digital world, may I propose to you that the digital world is center stage for modern-day society to build a Jesus brand. Like no other time in human history, we have the opportunity to leverage our individual, personal, and public digital platforms to build a better brand. A Jesus brand for *all to see*.

Reflection Questions

- Read Matthew 5–7. Has Jesus inspired you to live differently online? How, or why not?
- How can you use your digital platforms to share Jesus online? Share your ideas and stories at www.infobesity.ca.
- Out of the four engagement strategies of Jesus (helpful information, interactive information, inspired information, and invitational information), which one stands out to you the most? Why or why not?
- Starting today, how can you develop a Jesus brand online?

Conclusion

"We are in the middle of an information transfiguration."
—Quinten Shultz[1]

"We live in a world of information junk food."
—Marv Penner

The digital age is here to stay.

The last information revolution of the Gutenberg printing press was five hundred years ago; we are currently living in a new information revolution. It is a digital press. A Zuckerberg revolution.

Once the printing press was in full operation, information became accessible to society. Books, documents, and key forms of literature were available for the common good. Power structures changed. The common good of all became the focus. Modern forms of sciences, governments, and economics shifted. The Gutenberg press changed the course of human history.

In the same way, a Zuckerberg era has revolutionized information. Information has been flatlined. Information is accessible. Everyone and anyone can experience information. Information, like never before, has been released for the world to see. Just like the printing press, authority lines have shifted. Economics have changed. Communications have been revolutionized. Online content has become the place to find information.

Modern-day technology has created new pathways of communication, information, economics, and so much more. We have changed how we

1. Schultze, *Habits of the High-Tech Heart*, 16.

interact, conduct business, and connect with the world. Digital technology has redefined how we discover purpose and redefined how we engage with the world. We are navigating how to make a difference in our world in digital spaces. In addition to this, modern forms of information have changed how we learn, teach, communicate, and engage with each other.

As much as digital technologies have been a great advancement for humanity, research on digital information has shown negative consequences as well. *Infobesity*—the effects of unregulated and unmoderated forms of information from digital spaces—has caused mental health issues, modern-day loneliness, extreme hyper-individualism, personalization modes of truth, lower individual well-being, and violence towards institutional models of authority.

In a world of unlimited information, a wave of digital information will be moving from content-telling to story-telling. We simply cannot consume all the information online. In a world where five hundred years' worth of information has been downloaded to the internet in the span of two years, we will continue to be bombarded by *infobesity*.

Due to this, we are moving away from certain forms of empirical learning. The world is flowing from linear modes of learning to dialogue and networking. Even more so, society is experimenting with different models of learning. People are filtering learning through personal experiences, relational modes of thought, and personal happiness. This will have profound realities for followers of Jesus—if it hasn't already. In a world bombarded by *infobesity*, we have the unique responsibility to be redemptive in future modes of filtering information and learning.

In a world wrestling through modes of information from content-telling to story-telling, perhaps, as followers of Jesus, we can respond with story-sharing to reveal Truth to a world oversaturated with *infobesity*. As followers of Jesus, the human response to technology will repeat itself like the digital garden of old or seen with the timeless truths in the ancient selfie. Humanity has its limits.

In the creative pursuits of human history, we cannot create the Creator. Technology has its limits. As followers of Jesus, the principles of being Jesus in our world will remain. As technology changes at increasingly rapid rates, the desire to meet all of humans' needs and wants will be the motivation for the latest and greatest technological advancements in our society.

The concepts of human robotics, artificial intelligence, machine consciousness, genetic advancements, relational robots, pursuits to expand lifespan, to look younger longer, and to create cyborg memory canals will be the future realities of technology.

However, as illustrated throughout this book, the technological concepts of modern-day technicism are limited by the human condition in all of us. We are broken. We are flawed. We are empty without Jesus.

In particular, the latest technological structures of online access have seen these limitations. The causes of *infobesity* have had negative outcomes because technology cannot answer all of humanity's problems. Modern-day technology tries to grasp the fundamental questions of life: "What does it mean to be human? How can we create a human soul? How can we find meaning and purpose in a technological age?" These are questions technology has limited capacities to answer.

As followers of Jesus, it should be no surprise that these questions have been answered in the ancient ways of Jesus. He is the answer to the human condition. Jesus has answered the modern-day questions of life. Jesus is the answer to the nagging realities of purpose, meaning, and life on earth. He has answered the foundational questions of humanity.

He addresses our fears. He conquered death. He speaks into our hearts. He inspires us to accept the realities of our own limited weaknesses. He gives hope to the broken world. Jesus answers the pursuits of modern-day technicism.

As followers of Jesus living in a digital age, we have a unique opportunity to address *infobesity* with hope, purpose, and love in Jesus. We have the redemptive digital practices to provide a better way. We can live redemptively.

Online, we can practice the digital habits of Jesus and redeem a digital world for all to see. For all to see what it means to live free from *infobesity*. To reveal Jesus to a modern-day world struggling with *infobesity*.

This is how you and I can live in purpose.

CONCLUSION

Reflection Questions:

- What concepts in this book have encouraged you to redeem your digital practices and habits?
- How will you build a Jesus brand online?
- Share the *infobesity* self-assessment to your family and friends. It is a free resource for you.[2]

---

2. Access the infobesity assessment at www.andygabruch.com/redeemdigitalspaces. Use promo code DUCO.

Practical Infobesity Resources

Infobesity Resources for Parents

My name is Andy, and I am a parent living in a digital age.

As a parent of two preteens and two teenagers, I *know* how much is going on as a parent. There's school, sports, music lessons, events at your church or community. There's work, hobbies, constant birthday parties, and let's top it off with the distractions from our digital devices.

How do we—as parents—parent in a digital age?

How can we empower our children to make wise decisions with their digital practices?

How much time is too much time on our screens?

And how can we disciple our children with healthy digital habits?

In my experience as a pastor, in my own home as a parent, and in my doctoral research with George Fox University, I have seen how our digital devices have shaped our minds and relationships with others, our families, with Jesus, and even with ourselves.

If we had the opportunity to have a coffee together, I would recommend three important realities for parents parenting in a digital age—the first one is to regulate our digital devices, the second would be how to moderate digital consumption from our digital devices, and the third is how to redeem digital practices.

First, let's talk about the regulation of digital devices.

Studies reveal negative behaviors increase with increased digital consumption in our children.

These negative behaviors include irritability; including fits of anger, impatience, and meltdowns (because children—and adults alike—cannot process the enormous amounts of information they are bombarded with online), and this leads to a slowness to obey or listen to commands (because digital entertainment increases distractions and decreases retention in children and adults), and causes addictive decision-making processes (because, for example, software engineers have designed addictive behavior in digital spaces to be as flashy as slot machines in casinos) and children cannot cope with real-life situations.

This is why regulating digital devices is so important—because our governments and big tech companies don't. Even more so, studies reveal excessive screen time is linked to mental health issues, lack of personal coping skills, and relational isolationism.

In fact, according to child psychiatrist Dr. Dunckley, higher levels of digital consumption leas to what is termed "ESS," "electronic screen syndrome."[1]

In short, parents—like you and me—are the only regulating system for our children.

So, how can we take back our children from digital distractions?

How can we protect our children from ESS?

How can we parent well in a digital world? And, how can we help our children develop healthy digital habits?

Are you ready for this?! Let's jump into it . . .

Well, first, as parents, we need to regulate digital devices for our children. Experts suggest digital consumption should be no more than two hours per day and digital devices should not be picked up within two hours before bedtime and two hours after waking up.

---

1. DeFrank, *Digital Detox*, loc. 30, Kindle.

According to the same experts, digital devices should be charged in a common room in your home, like the living room or rec room (not in bedrooms) and should not be used during dinnertime or in the bathroom.

The second way you can regulate digital devices in your home is to take a weekly digital sabbath. Take a day to connect with each other by disconnecting your digital devices as a family. You might be asking yourself, "Really, Andy?! Does this even work? Is this even possible?"

Yes, it does, and it is.

Take your children out for a hike or a night out on the town. It could include going out for bowling, or go-karts, or it could be a date night with your kids.

Even in your own home, get them to read a physical book rather than an electronic one. *Why* is that? Because studies conclude children can retain higher rates of learning from a physical book than an electronic one.

Or simply play a board game together.

Digital sabbaths are a game changer because they get your children off their digital devices and reset them to how God has designed them to be.

You might get the infamous, "Yeah, but I'm bored!" response, but it is a good thing.

As sabbaths are meant to reset us to God in rest and renewal, a digital sabbath resets us to be human.

Being bored allows our children to reset their imaginations, stimulates their brain (and doesn't numb them out with cheap online entertainment), and rebuilds face-to-face social skills. Being bored is not a problem but an opportunity and realigns children to reset what is normal in real life.

For starters, I would strongly encourage building a "fun list" with your family. Allow your children to develop a list of fun activities to do together during your digital sabbath.

And, at the end of the day, recap with your family.

How did your digital sabbath go?

What excited them?

What fun activities did you do?

And if you'd like, record your experiences with a digital sabbath journal. Jot ideas down and share the benefits of disconnecting digitally to connect relationally with each other.

And if a digital weekly sabbath seems far-fetched, then start with a digital detox for a few hours.

Last, a great way to regulate digital devices is to have a family technology "rule."

For my family, our technology rule is to approach technology as a tool for real life, not to replace real life. Technology is meant to connect us with each other, not to isolate us from each other. Technology is to work for us, not to enslave us, and when we are stressed out, we won't go to screens and reels, but take a break in nature with God.

To recap, I encourage you as parents to limit use of digital devices to two hours a day (excluding school or work), take a weekly digital sabbath (or a few hours a week), create a "fun list" together, and develop a technology "rule of life."

This will help shape you, your family, and your children to develop healthy digital habits.

Second, I would recommend moderation of digital consumption. What your children are watching, or being entertained with, and accessing online should be moderated by *you*.

This helps our children filter through what is godly or distracting, what is beneficially or harmful, and what is true or fake.

As parents, we have the authority to filter through what our children are watching.

The number one way to moderate digital consumption is through healthy relationships. I love how Josh McDowell puts it. He says, "Rules without relationship leads to rebellion." It is so true!

In other words, build safe places where conversations can thrive. Healthy conversations are vital for healthy digital practices to prosper. Lead by example. Practice boundaries around your own digital practices and habits. Lead with digital-free zones in your home. Frontload responses with your children and students. Give them advanced warning to detox them from their digital practices and habits. In our home, this included the practice of countdowns. We would give our children a ten-minute countdown, a five-minute countdown, and then a two-minute countdown. This allowed our children to prepare for their digital detox, especially if you implement the 2-2-2 principle discussed throughout this book.

I would recommend having digital-free zones, such as the dinner table or family car rides. Ask good questions, listen to your kids, and educate your children on the awareness of their digital devices at dinnertime and on the way to soccer practice.

After a decade of research, digital spaces have not owned up to what they have promised. More and more children, students, and families are experiencing the harmful effects of information overload living in a digital world. We need to educate our families through healthy conversations and relationships.

Develop a reward system. If you home has chores or homework or duties to accomplish, provide a collaborative method within your home on rewarding your family with digital activity. Use pre-programmed communication with your family as digital devices are not available until chores and schoolwork is completed.

Review with your family over quality conversations about their digital practices and habits. In our home, we can have these quality conversations over weekly date nights. It is the opportunity to reconnect with our children one-on-one as parents. If I was honest with you, this has been the best practice we have implemented into our home after the pandemic.

Second, moderate digital consumption through intentional spaces. Be the "home" your children can invite their friends to. Have family get-togethers with their friends, cook together, plan activities—such as a jog, or walk, or bike ride—together, have games nights, enjoy a LEGO building contest, do activities "offline," and be the hub your children can invite their friends to.

You might be saying to yourself, "Man, Andy, that sound expensive! Do you know how much my kids eat?"

Yes, there is a cost (and I get it), but it is worth the investment.

Jean Twenge, a San Diego State University psychologist and professor, puts it this way: "Children who spend more time on screen activities are more likely to be unhappy than those who spend more time on non-screen activities." In short, 54 percent of children who are online are more unhappy compared to those whose activities are offline.

Third, moderating digital consumption is building a long-term plan for your family. Depending on the age of your children, I'd recommend building a personalized digital plan with each of them. Practically speaking, here are some personalized ideas based on the age and stage of your child. You can also access a free personalized plan and ideas on my website at andygabruch.com.

Parenting children (ages 2–9)

For children between the ages of two and nine years, we would recommend:

- Limiting digital consumption to thirty minutes to two hours a day (excluding school),
- Digital devices are *always* in public spaces (in the home),
- No social media platforms,
- Parents monitor digital consumption, whether for videos, gaming, or connecting with family and friends,
- Educating your children on digital spaces and places, and
- Practice weekly digital sabbaths as a family.

Parenting preteens (ages 10–12)

For children ages between ten and twelve years old, we would recommend:

- Limiting digital consumption to two hours a day (excluding school),
- Developing a rule of technology for your children,

- No social media platforms (as social media platforms prohibit children under thirteen, unless parents are monitoring those platforms),
- No personal digital devices (family devices only),
- Using parental settings on all devices,
- Creating a "fun list" with your children,
- Educating your preteens on the harmful effects of digital spaces and places, and
- Practicing weekly digital sabbaths as a family.

Parenting teenagers (ages 13–19)

And for teenagers between thirteen and eighteen we would recommend:

- Moderating digital consumption to two hours a day (excluding school and work),
- Developing a personal plan with your child on the rule of technology and a "fun list" for non-screen activities,
- Creating weekly digital-free spaces and places for friends and conversations to thrive,
- Sharing peer and/or family stories on the realities of information overload, and
- Practicing weekly digital sabbaths with your teens.

And last, this leads me to the most important aspect of our study on *infobesity*—it is to redeem digital practices.

You might be reading this and saying to yourself, "There is *no* way this is going to work with my family," or "We are just too connected to our digital devices."

I want to encourage you, whatever age or stage your family is in or whatever level of digital consumption you are encountering, these practices will help you redeem your family and children to use their digital practices in the view of Jesus rather than the digital pressures around them.

If you and/or your family member is addicted to your digital devices, here is some practical advice.

First, get a dumb phone. Get a phone you can only text and take calls. This will help regulate and moderate digital information; and yet will still let you connect with family and friends.

Second, take a digital sabbatical (not just a weekly sabbath) with a thirty-day, sixty-day, or a ninety-day detox from digital consumption. This excludes work and education, of course, but it will reset you or your family. Use a journal to record your experiences.

Third, talk to a professional. Counsellors and psychologists alike are gradually focusing on helping parents and children around digital addiction.

Last, pray and plan. Allow God to guide you and give you strength. You are the parent. You are the one to regulate, and educate, and moderate healthy digital habits for you and your family.

You've got this, friend!

We have *infobesity* resources, plans, ideas, and a technology "way of life" templates on my website. Feel free to interact with me anytime at andygabruch.com.

And last, before you go back to your busy and crazy life parenting your child and family in a digital age, ask yourself, what is *one* takeaway from this book that stood out to you, and how are you going to implement it with your family?

Cheering you on, friend!

Infobesity Resources for Students

For the first time in history, you are the first generation to be a digital native. What this means is you have been born into a world with digital devices. Since your entry into this world, digital information has been at your fingertips. You can game, work, study, play, interact, live, and sleep with your digital device.

When COVID-19 hit, you had unlimited access to screens. You have been wired to be entertained. You have been shaped to live online. And whether you like it or not, your digital practices and habits are shaping you in positive and negative ways. The same device you work with, play video games on, interact with family and friends on, and even study on is the same device—as we have seen with the research on *infobesity*—that can entice you with cheap entertainment, modern-day distractions, and damaging dopamine feedback loops.

Without regulating your digital habits and moderating your digital practices, your overall well-being will decrease over time. The evidence is out there. Mental health issues rise, relational skills decrease, coping skills for everyday life are stifled, and mental cognition is reduced as digital consumption increases.

You are not created to be digital.

Loneliness, mental health concerns, isolationism, lack of mental retention, and sleep issues are all linked to moderate to high levels of digital consumption I call *infobesity*.

So, what do we do about it?

If you have interacted throughout this book, great! I hope you can take some of the principles and practices to become a well-equipped follower of Jesus in a digital world. If you haven't, we either take the extremes of rejecting digital spaces altogether or receiving digital spaces with little thought of the effects of *infobesity* in our lives.

Developed in conversations with students across the nation, including preteens, teenagers, and university students, the practical recommendations we have for you are to not to limit you but to help you thrive as a follower of Jesus. Growing, living, and breathing God's divine purposes for your life in a digital world.

Here are some key insights for you. I hope you can share these digital practices with your friends too.

Develop a Digital Sabbath

Take a break from your digital connections. Even if work or school is a part of your online activity, taking a daily break and weekly digital sabbath from your digital devices will become important to reconnect with God.

When you reconnect with God your purpose becomes clear, your dopamine levels reset, your brain function increases, and your overall well-being with thrive. We have provided a few suggestions on how to develop a digital sabbath for you.

Moderate

- Charge your phone in a public place at night. Studies continue to reveal that lack of sleep, bouts of insomnia, and screen fatigue are linked to digital device activity at night. This can have negative effects on your cognitive retention, mood swings, and daily overall well-being.[2] Charge your phone in the living room rather than your bedroom,

- Connect with God with a hardcopy devotional or reading of the Bible. Again, the latest research has concluded, even though there are hundreds of thousands of digital devices for the modern-day classroom, hardcopy reading has a higher retention of learning than digital avenues. This has been explained through the ability of brain volumes of information retention. Anything over the brain channel of information is lost due to information overload. This can cause fits of anger, irritability, and loss of cognitive reasoning—simply put, the brain will shut down. According to cognitive neurosciences, the brain can consume approximately one conversation at a time or one book at a time. Beyond that, the brain struggles to retain information and switches to a filtering system of information through the importance of the individual called attention filter.[3]

---

2. Crouch and Crouch, *My Tech-Wise Life*, loc. 165, Kindle.
3. Levitin, *Organized Mind*, loc. 7564, Kindle.

Regulate

- Track your online activity and screenshot it. Try to keep a journal to track your online trends and themes, and how to keep your digital consumption to no more than two hours a day (excluding work and education). Over a ten-year linear period over multiple studies in the United States, England, Australia, Iceland, Canada, Sweden, and Finland, both quantified and qualified research approaches revealed the negative effects of information overload after two hours of digital usage.[4] A US university study suggests no more than thirty minutes of social media usage.[5]
- Put your notifications on silent so the pings, dings, and zings from your digital device won't distract you.
- Allow a friend or pastor or parent to have access to your digital device at any time. Share your password, your social media accounts, and files to someone to access at their discretion. Again, this isn't about judgement as much as friendship and accountability to bring out the best in you.

Listen

- Quiet yourself with God by reconnecting with him in Creation. Go for a walk, go to the park, hike a mountain, find an activity you enjoy. With this, it will help you reconnect with God and develop healthy levels of dopamine. Activity studies recommend one hour of activity for students and thirty minutes of activity for adults. Activity creates healthy modes of dopamine (feelings of happiness), and oxytocin (feelings of human connection) resets when we are physically active. Furthermore, activity reduces social anxiety, helps us filter through positive and negative feelings, and increases overall well-being.
- Listen to worship music in your room. Fill your mind with good and wholesome things. Again, studies reveal the transformation of our minds start with what we listen to. Digital spaces are designed, at their core, to distract, entertain, and entice us to our human self-indulgences. Due to this, we experience information overload. Allowing

---

4. Haidt et al., "Social Media and Mental Health," 244.
5. Hunt et al., "No More FOMO," para. 4.

worship in your life will reset your brain towards the things of God and develop healthy practices and habits with your digital device.

Redeem Digital Spaces

REDEEM YOUR DIGITAL PRACTICES

If you are currently over moderate levels of digital consumption (over two hours a day, excluding work and school), then we need to find practical ways to decrease your digital practices for your own well-being. We call these redemptive practices. As mentioned in this resource page, all these practices will help redeem your digital practices—but don't do it alone. Allow others in your life so that infobesity does not lead your life, but the Savior does.

With that said, here are some key and practical ways to redeem your digital practices:

- Moderate digital consumption to two hours per day (excluding school and work),
- Developing a personal plan around the rule of technology,
- Start a non-screen "fun list" each day,
- Creating weekly digital-free spaces and places for friends and conversations to thrive,
- Practice weekly digital sabbaths,
- Develop a Jesus brand,
- Get a dumb phone to stay connected but not distracted,
- Talk to a pastor or counsellor for professional help (for higher levels of infobesity).

DEVELOP AN *INFOBESITY* GROUP

- Build a community of like-minded people to discuss how to moderate, regulate, and redeem digital spaces face-to-face in real time. Our encouragement would be a small group no more than seven people. Studies have revealed, as mentioned in this book, anything over seven people face-to-face results in competing voices. This could include your peers, friends, a mentor, or youth pastor. You can find practical *infobesity* resources on how to develop an *infobesity* group at www.andygabruch.com.

Get Involved in a Local Church

- We are designed for community, for face-to-face interaction, for belonging and friendship. We would encourage you not to just attend a youth ministry or young adult ministry or a local church but to get involved. Grow in your relationship with God, in practical ways—as the Search Institute would recommend—to exercise your gifts, passions, and abilities in ways to help others. Talk to your youth leader or pastor on how to get involved. It could change your life, for the better.
- Studies out of the United Kingdom are revealing the number one way to tackle modern-day loneliness and lack of personal purpose is to serve others in practical ways. The local church is a great place to combat modern-day loneliness.

Develop a Jesus Brand

- Share a weekly story on your socials of how Jesus has been EPIC in your life
- Use interactive questions to share your faith. Questions like:
    - "How can I pray for you?"
    - "If Jesus could answer one question for you, what would be your question?"
    - "Hey, want to come to youth group with me? There's free pizza!"
    - "What do you think about Jesus?"
    - Quote your favorite verse and ask, "What do you think about this verse?"
    - "How has Jesus been real with you this week?"
    - "Want to meet up at a local coffee shop and read the proverb of the day together?"
    - "Want to start an *infobesity* group online?"

- Share helpful, not harmful or hurtful, information online. Information that is helpful can include encouraging notes, prayer texts, quoting Scripture, or sharing a fun digital-free activity.
- Invite a mentor to cheer you on as you develop healthy personal digital habits and practices.
- Ask Jesus in prayer for creative ways to use digital spaces and places for "everyone to see."
- Ask Jesus to free you from digital sins (moderate to high digital consumption, engaging with hurtful or harmful or sexualized information, sharing misinformation, online bullying).

I hope these recommendations, based on the latest research, for digital regulation, moderation, and redemption of digital spaces and places will empower you to live life to the full. Of course, video games and interacting with online content and platforms are positive and rewarding, if we practice use of digital spaces in light of who Jesus is rather than our own self-indulgences and selfishness.

In addition to this, feel free to stay connected with us as we develop *infobesity* connecting points, technology think tanks, and help us create innovative ways of how to be followers of Jesus in a digital world.

Cheers!

Infobesity Resources for Pastors

I will never forget the day when one of my student youth leaders confessed a digital sin to me. It was on the heels of one of the best youth events I have ever led.

We ran out of Bibles. Dozens of students gave their lives to Jesus. Others requested to take their next step of faith in water baptism. We packed out the building with students from across the city. It was a memory I will never forget.

Unfortunately, this twelfth-grade student confessed to sending inappropriate pictures to a student who was at our youth event that night. He had never participated in one of our events before, but my twelfth-grade leader felt deep feelings of shame and overwhelming guilt like she never experienced before.

She had memorized Scripture. She has been on short-term mission trips. She was one of the core reasons our youth ministry was growing. During the night, of course, her digital sin wasn't public or known to anyone. That is what makes unregulated digital practices so dangerous. Digital sins are private. But, as this guy came to our event that night, conviction flooded her soul. She didn't know how to respond.

In her pain, she came to me. She confessed what happened. At the end of the youth night, as we had a team debrief, she shared how her digital sins happened in the blink of an eye, the snap of a picture in a moment of human weakness.

I am assuming you have experienced the same stories in your church. As we live in a digital world of endless cheap entertainment, instant accessibility, and self-indulgent practices, my twelfth-grade leader sent five pictures in the span of forty-five seconds from her private bathroom to a relatively unknown stranger from school.

I realized one of the highlights of my ministerial life was being matched with a current low. I understood that night the deep disconnect in how I had prepared my youth ministry team to be disciples living in a digital age. Over the course of time, I have been teaching, training, and leading churches, denominations, and youth ministries to develop discipleship methods for a digital world. I have taught them the dangers to *infobesity*, and how to practice digital discipleship, including personal digital practices and habits and how to redeem digital spaces. The discipleship processes in our culture are changing. Since then, I have researched, studied, read, and kept up with the latest findings on digital information. I have gone through a doctoral research process to discern how to redeem digital spaces as followers of Jesus. Since 2010, I have been teaching and leading on the topic of *infobesity* helping spiritual leaders and pastors realize their need to shepherd their flock in digital spaces.

I have worked with hundreds of parents and families, travelled the world testing the concepts of modern-day *infobesity* in local churches and with denominational leaders. Across the world, *infobesity* has been shaping our flocks more than we know.

Based on our research, less than 10 percent of pastors teach on digital discipleship. In some cases, pastors don't know how to teach on how to be followers of Jesus online. In other cases, pastors expect discipleship practices to include their congregants' digital practices. However, the research concludes this is not the case.

Inter-congregant fighting, online bullying, personalization of theology, and/or congregation unhappiness have all been included in the stories shared with me. Maybe you are reading this and you have experienced the same. How do we help our congregations to be mature followers of Jesus in digital spaces?

I have heard stories of congregants airing out their discontent for their pastor or worship experience online. Others have shared hateful information about fellow congregants. Some, who are elevated to leadership share their self-indulgent experiences online, sabotaging their trusted influence in their church. Their faith is questioned and the church leadership seems untrustworthy. This is happening at a rapid rate in our infobese world.

Add a global pandemic where churches had to become digitalized in a matter of moments, and local church leaders and pastors are on a microscope. On a digital scale, pastors have been ill-equipped to deal with the realities of *infobesity* in a digital world.

As we have journeyed throughout this book, the heart of the conversation is to redeem digital spaces and places as followers of Jesus. I hope these practical ideas can help you pastor and shepherd a community living, breathing, working, and influenced by digital spaces.

Teach on Digital Spaces

- Start an *infobesity* small group(s) initiative to go through the *infobesity* thirty-day challenge,
- Teach on the effects of *infobesity* on faith in the family,
- Start a parent's small group to help navigate their children living in a digital age,
- Do a sermon series on sections of the book, how to understand digital spaces, respond to digital spaces, and how to redeem digital spaces,

- Develop a digital think tank to address the trends and themes of digital spaces,
- Experiment with new modes of communication interacting with digital platforms and/or questions in your message content.

Lead by Personal Example

- Use your digital platforms as an opportunity to build a Jesus brand (not your own ministerial brand),
- Share stories of God working in and through your congregation to develop healthy and redemptive digital practices and habits,
- Be a part of the Technology Think Tank with DUCO. Find details for those events at www.andygabruch.com.

Develop a Ministerial Engagement Strategy

- Create a digital creative team,
- Develop a plan with the engagement factors of Jesus to share online content and influence. These people should be digital natives and/or have experience with developing digital content,
- Research the latest Christian resources on how to engage the world online. Please note: this is not just about sharing content online but ways to engage and connect online as well. Studies reveal 50 percent (and increasing) of people will join your church online before they ever walk into your physical buildings and services,

Determine a Discipleship Model Including Digital Practices and Habits

- Promote the *infobesity* self-assessment for congregants to interact with and implement,
- Implement the *infobesity* model of how to process online information for congregants,[6]

---

6. See Gabruch, "Infobesity," 33.

- Digital discipleship coaching. For implementation, coaching options, and contextualized *infobesity* models, please contact duco@andygabruch.com.

Infobesity Thirty-Day Personal Challenge

Welcome to the *Infobesity* Personal Challenge! I am excited to journey with you.

In conversations with various youth leaders, parents, and churches alike, it became imperatively clear people are looking for practical steps on how to address the effects of *infobesity* in their homes, hearts, local churches, and communities.

Due to this, I have developed a personal *infobesity* challenge. The challenge is to help digital users understand, respond to, and redeem their digital practices.

To make the most out of this journey, I would encourage you to invite someone to walk with you on this journey. One of the reoccurring issues with *infobesity* is the isolationism and privatization of digital practices and habits. To invite a friend, colleague, trusted mentor, or counsellor will help empower you to address the level of *infobesity* you are currently facing would be beneficial.

If you cannot find someone safe enough to walk with you, feel free to join one of the reoccurring *infobesity* groups we offer online at www.infobesity.ca. You can find all the details there.

The *Infobesity* Thirty-Day Personal Challenge is designed to concentrate on the following:

Week One focuses on understanding your digital practices and habits.

Week Two focuses on how to practically respond to your digital practices and habits.

Week Three focuses on how to redeem digital practices and align your discipleship journey with Jesus.

Week four focuses on how to build a Jesus brand online for the world to see Jesus.

If you have any questions or comments about the *Infobesity* Thirty-Day Personal Challenge, or want to share your personal *infobesity* challenge story, please reach out to us at www.infobesity.ca. We would love for you to share your story.

Thank you, and enjoy the journey, friend!

Week One: Understanding Your Digital Practices

Day One: Take the *Infobesity* Assessment at www.andygabruch.com/redeemdigitalspaces.

Day Two: Limit social media consumption to two hours or less a day (for entertainment, digital consumption, and social media).

Day Three: Invite someone to walk with you in developing healthy digital habits.

Day Four: Screenshot your daily digital consumption to build self-awareness of your digital practices. Share your screenshots with someone.

Day Five: Plan non-screen activities every day. For students, this would include one hour of activity. For adults, this would include thirty minutes of activity. Take digital breaks for every one hour if you work online and/or are in digital spaces for education.

Day Six: Read and reflect on Scripture from your *Infobesity* Assessment. Apply the Scripture readings to your digital practices and habits.

Day Seven: Start an *infobesity* journal. Reflect on your mental health well-being. Has your personal well-being increased as your digital practices decreased? Share your experiences with a friend or at www.infobesity.ca.

Week Two: Responding to Your Digital Practices

Day One: How has your social media practices shaped you more than Scripture? Share your experiences in your *infobesity* journal. What practical steps can you take to make sure Scripture shapes you more than your socials?

Day Two: Discern and filter online information through the lenses of Truth. How will you do this? Share your experiences in your *infobesity* journal.

Day Three: Develop a twenty-four–hour digital sabbath. Disconnect from the digital Trinity to reconnect with the divine. If this seems unreasonable, start with a digital detox. We'd encourage a digital detox of four hours per day. This could include an afternoon detox or an evening detox—whatever you prefer.

Day Four: Develop a technological "Way of Life." Practice technology as a tool for everyday life not an idol overtaking your life.

Day Five: Confess your digital sins. Allow Jesus to heal you, set your free, and listen to his wisdom on how to address digital sins.

Day Six: Ban digital consumption two hours before bed and two hours after you wake up. Practice resetting your mind for the next day and to prepare for the following day. Limit yourself to two hours of digital activity per day (excluding work and education). Use this time to read and write. Engage in meaningful conversations, and/or use your time to connect with God. We call this the digital practice the 2-2-2 principle.

Day Seven: Share your passwords and accounts with a trusted friend or family member. Keep digital practices and habits in the light. This can be anyone you trust, including a mentor, parent, spouse, or youth worker/pastor. This will limit the temptation for digital sins to rise and addiction to set in.

Week Three: Redeeming Your Digital Practices

Day One: Develop an *infobesity* group. Walk in a covenantal community and practice the redemptive habits suggested in the book (discussing Week One and Week Two of the *Infobesity* Thirty-Day Personal Challenge).

Day Two: Delete social media platforms which have been harmful, hurtful, and/or hateful towards your personal well-being. Redeem social relationship with others in digital spaces.

Day Three: Practice digital usage through the lens of tekton rather than technicism. Explore how your digital practices have shifting through the lens of Jesus being Truth. Write down your experiences in your *infobesity* journal.

Day Four: Continue to develop digital-free zones. This should include the dinner table, driving (even though most of us still do this), before and after bedtime, date nights with your significant other (unless consented to by your significant other), bathrooms, bedrooms (for children), and digital-free activities you decide.

Day Five: Silent notifications during focused hours of work. This will limit distractions and unproductivity in your life.

Day Six: Move towards a digital detox every day (including a digital sabbath every week). For example, limit blue screen intake during the night and/or buy blue blocker glasses for digital self-care. Limit digital consumption during your Sunday worship experiences.

Day Seven: Limit selfies to seven per week (or less). This way, you can focus on your own well-being, including others around you.

Week Four: Developing a Jesus Brand Online

Day One: Develop a plan to leverage your personal social media platforms to share Jesus online.

Day Two: Share a short video or image of an EPIC story you have had with Jesus this week.

Day Three: Invite your social media community to your youth ministry, small group, or church.

Day Four: Ask engaging questions about faith, life, and purpose in digital spaces. Develop interactive discussions with those on your digital platforms.

Day Five: Ask for prayer requests. Share prayer requests. Allow your social media platforms to be a place of spiritual healing and safety. Pray for others. Pray with others. Allow social media users to express their needs to you as you pray for them and with them.

Day Six: Facilitate an *infobesity* group with your friends, family, parents, or with your church community to go through the *Infobesity* Thirty-Day Personal Challenge.

Day Seven: Ask Jesus to give you practical wisdom, insight, and innovation on how to improve your personal digital practices and habits to build a Jesus brand online.

Technology "Way of Life" Template for Individuals

Technology "Way Of Life" Template for Families

Sample Infobesity Self-Assessment Infographic

You may be experiencing physical symptoms of digital information overload. These symptoms can include mild sleeping disorders, fatigue, distractions from work or school, a lack of motivation in your life, and physical comparisons.
If not addressed, you may experience stress-related diseases such as sleeping disorders, obesity, and/or hypertension. Extreme cases would include tourette's- like symptoms, brain fog, and/or eye strain causing underdeveloped eyesight
(in preadolescents).

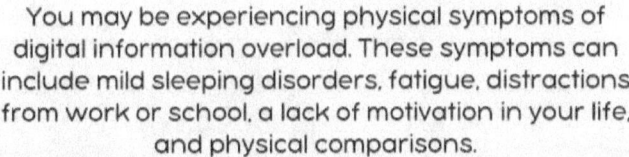

Limit your digital usage 2 hours before bed and after you wake up.

Personalize your digital device settings to mute notifications to decrease distractions throughout the day.

Next Steps

Limit your digital usage to 2 hours/day for entertainment, social media consumption, and online information.

Turn your phone off and/or on mute during meals with your family and/or friends.

Silence your phone when you are driving, sleeping, and at the dinner table to minimize distractions.

Plan for 30 minutes of activity per day (walk, run, hike)

Follow-Up Resources

We check our digital devices over 18500 times/year and is equivalent to once every 4.3 minutes (12 Ways Your Phone is Changing You, Tony Reinke)

College students waste 20% of class time tinkering on a digital device
(Digital Distraction in Class Is on the Rise, Leslie Reed)

Access the *Infobesity* Self-Assessment

As a part of purchasing this book, you have complimentary access to the Infobesity Self-Assessment Tool at www.andygabruch.com/redeemdigitalspaces

Password - DUCO

Bibliography

Adamson, Dave. *MetaChurch: How to Use Digital Ministry to Reach People and Make Disciples*. Cumming, GA: Orange, 2022.
AFP. "Selfies Kill More People than Shark Attacks, Study Finds." *CTV News*, June 27, 2019. https://www.ctvnews.ca/world/selfies-kill-more-people-than-shark-attacks-study-finds-1.4484691?cache=pawumraq.
"AI Expert David Levy Says a Human Will Marry a Robot by 2050." *CBC Radio*, January 6, 2017. https://www.cbc.ca/radio/day6/episode-319-becoming-kevin-o-leary-saving-shaker-music-google-renewables-marrying-robots-and-more-1.3921088/a-i-expert-david-levy-says-a-human-will-marry-a-robot-by-2050-1.3921101.
Alexander, Calah. "There's No Quick Fix for Loneliness, but Turning Off the AC Is a Start." *Aleteia*, January 31, 2018. https://aleteia.org/2018/01/31/theres-no-quick-fix-for-loneliness-but-turning-off-the-ac-is-a-start.
Alter, Adam. *Irresistible: The Rise of Addictive Technology and the Business of Keeping Us Hooked*. New York: Penguin, 2017.
Ambrosino, Brandon. "Don't Celebrate Faith Goldy's Facebook Ban. Be Concerned About What's Next." *Globe and Mail*, April 10, 2019. https://www.theglobeandmail.com/opinion/article-dont-celebrate-faith-goldys-facebook-ban-be-concerned-about-whats.
Anderson, Monica, and Jingjing Jiang. "Teens' Social Media Habits and Experiences." *Pew Research Center*, November 28, 2018. file:///Users/richardjhiemstra/Downloads/PI_2018.11.28_teens-social-media_FINAL4.pdf.
———. "Teens, Social Media, and Technology 2018." *Pew Research Center*, May 31, 2018. http://assets.pewresearch.org/wp-content/uploads/sites/14/2018/05/31102617/PI_2018.05.31_TeensTech_FINAL.pdf.
Anderson, Monica, and Andrew Perrin. "Tech Adoption Climbs Among Older Adults." *Pew Research Center*, May 17, 2017. https://www.pewresearch.org/internet/2017/05/17/tech-adoption-climbs-among-older-adults.
Angus Reid Institute. "Canadians Offer Little Sympathy for Parents (Candy) Crushed by Kids' In-App Purchases." *Angus Reid Institute*, October 24, 2017. http://angusreid.org/in-app-purchase-policy.

———. "Digital Dopamine: Half of Canadian Parents Concerned Their Child Spends Too Much Time on Their Devices." *Angus Reid Institute*, September 3, 2019. http://angusreid.org/screen-time-kids.

———. "A Portrait of Social Isolation and Loneliness in Canada Today." *Angus Reid Institute*, June 17, 2019. http://angusreid.org/social-isolation-loneliness-canada.

———. "Trolls and Tribulations: One-in-Four Canadians Say They're Being Harassed on Social Media." *Angus Reid Institute*, October 21, 2016. https://angusreid.org/wp-content/uploads/2016/10/2016.10.04-Social-Media.pdf.

Arndt, W., et al. *A Greek-English Lexicon of the New Testament and Other Early Christian Literature*. 3rd ed. Chicago: University of Chicago Press, 2000.

Aslam, Salman. "Snapchat by the Numbers (2018): Stats, Demographics & Fun Facts." *Omnicore*, February 13, 2018. https://www.omnicoreagency.com/snapchat-statistics.

Associated Press. "US Senators Grill Facebook Exec About Instagram's Potential Harm to Teen Girls." *CBC.ca*, September 30, 2021. https://www.cbc.ca/news/world/facebook-instagram-harms-teens-senate-hearings-1.6195604.

Auxier, Brooke, and Monica Anderson. "Social Media Use in 2021." *Pew Research Center*, April 7, 2021. https://www.pewresearch.org/internet/2021/04/07/social-media-use-in-2021.

Bajarin, Ben. "Apple's Penchant for Consumer Security." *Tech.pinions*, April 18, 2016. https://techpinions.com/apples-penchant-for-consumer-security/45122.

Balakrishnan, Anita. "How Many Users Does Facebook Have? Two Billion a Month, CEO Mark Zuckerberg Says." *CNBC*, June 27, 2017. https://www.cnbc.com/2017/06/27/how-many-users-does-facebook-have-2-billion-a-month-ceo-mark-zuckerberg-says.html.

Balkissoon, Denise. "Boycotting Twitter? Why Breaking Our Social Media Addiction Is Healthy (And So Hard)." *Globe and Mail*, October 12, 2017. https://www.theglobeandmail.com/opinion/today-women-are-boycotting-twitter-heres-why/article36570399.

Baraniuk, Chris. "Facebook Plans Major Changes to News Feed." *BBC News*, January 11, 2018. http://www.bbc.com/news/technology-42657621.

Basu, Tanya. "Teens Are Anxious and Depressed After Three Hours a Day on Social Media." *MIT Technology Review*, September 11, 2019. https://www.technologyreview.com/f/614297/teens-are-anxious-and-depressed-after-three-hours-a-day-on-social-media.

"BC Mayor Goes Facebook-Free to Preserve Mental Health, Find Better Ways to Connect with Their Community." *CBC News*, February 19, 2022. https://www.cbc.ca/news/canada/british-columbia/facebook-free-february-interior-mayors-1.6356105.

Beck, Julie. "The Complex Psychology of Why People Like Things." *Atlantic*, May 16, 2016. https://www.theatlantic.com/science/archive/2016/05/the-complex-psychology-of-why-people-like-things/482196.

Bedingfield, Will. "How Social Media Broke Britain." *Wired UK*, October 1, 2020. https://www.wired.co.uk/article/this-is-not-normal-review.

Bell, Victoria. "Alexa Is Listening to Your Conversations: Web Giant Admits Clips Are Analysed by Amazon Workers—Including Your Most Intimate Moments." *Daily Mail*, April 11, 2019. https://www.dailymail.co.uk/sciencetech/article-6910791/Alexa-listening-conversations.html.

Belz, Emily. "Digital Life After Death: Few People Are Prepared Emotionally or Practically for Handling Social Media and Other Digital Accounts After a Loved One Dies." *World*, October 23, 2019. https://world.wng.org/2019/10/digital_life_after_death.

Berger, Michele W. "Social Media Use Increases Depression and Loneliness: In the First Experimental Study of Facebook, Snapchat, and Instagram Use, Psychologist Melissa G. Hunt Showed a Causal Link Between Time Spent on the Platforms and Decreased Well-Being." *Penn Today*, November 9, 2018. https://penntoday.upenn.edu/news/social-media-use-increases-depression-and-loneliness.

Berryman, Chloe, et al. "Social Media Use and Mental Health among Young Adults." *Psychiatric Quarterly* 89.2 (2018) 307–14.

Blevis, Mark, and David Coletto. "Matters of Opinion 2017: Eight Things We Learned About Politics, the News, and the Internet." *Abacus Data*, February 7, 2017. http://abacusdata.ca/matters-of-opinion-2017-8-things-we-learned-about-politics-the-news-and-the-internet.

Bogost, Ian. "I Tried to Limit My Screen Time: It Didn't Go Well." *Atlantic*, September 5, 2019. https://www.theatlantic.com/technology/archive/2019/09/why-apple-screen-time-mostly-makes-things-worse/597397.

Borgmann, Albert. *Power Failure: Christianity in the Culture of Technology*. Grand Rapids: Brazos, 2003.

Bowles, Nellie. "Human Contact Is Now a Luxury Good." *New York Times*, March 23, 2019. https://www.nytimes.com/2019/03/23/sunday-review/human-contact-luxury-screens.html.

Brandon, John. "New Survey Says We're Spending Seven Hours Per Day Consuming Online Media." *Forbes*, November 17, 2020. https://www.forbes.com/sites/johnbbrandon/2020/11/17/new-survey-says-were-spending-7-hours-per-day-consuming-online-media/?sh=13ba27dc6b46.

Brocklehurst, Sean. "Malcolm Gladwell on Why Watching Someone's Behavior Is Such a Flawed Way to Detect Liars." *CBC News*, October 20, 2019. https://www.cbc.ca/news/canada/malcolm-gladwell-interview-1.5303203.

Brooks, David. "The Shame Culture." *New York Times*, March 15, 2016. https://www.nytimes.com/2016/03/15/opinion/the-shame-culture.html.

Brown, Desmond. "Cellphone Ban in Ontario Classrooms Starts Today." *CBC*, November 3, 2019. https://www.cbc.ca/news/canada/toronto/cellphone-ban-ontario-classrooms-1.5346207.

Broz, Matic. "Selfie Statistics, Demographics, and Fun Facts (2024)." *Photutorial*, May 31, 2024. https://photutorial.com/selfie-statistics.

Buck, Naomi. "Hold the Phone: Cellphones Have Taken over Our Schools, and It's Been a Disaster. Now That We Know the Effects Screens Have on Our Children, We Need a New Approach." *Globe and Mail*, September 1, 2023. https://www.theglobeandmail.com/opinion/article-cellphones-have-taken-over-our-schools-and-its-been-a-disaster-for-our.

Buckner, Dianne. "Smartphones, Other Distractions Can Be More Deadly than Impaired Driving, Data Suggests." *CBC News*, October 29, 2019. https://www.cbc.ca/news/business/driving-distracted-worse-than-impaired-1.5330396.

Campbell, Heidi A., and Stephen Garner. *Networked Theology: Negotiating Faith in Digital Culture*. Grand Rapids: Baker Academic, 2016.

BIBLIOGRAPHY

"Canadians Still Driving Distracted in Alarming Numbers." *InsuranceHotline.com*, April 11, 2019. https://www.insurancehotline.com/resources/canadians-still-driving-distracted-in-alarming-numbers.

Cara, Ed. "The Internet Has Made Americans More Casual About Religion." *Gizmodo*, January 18, 2018. https://gizmodo.com/the-internet-has-made-americans-more-casual-about-relig-1822158186.

Castillo, Evan. "These Colleges Just Banned TikTok." *BestColleges*, April 24, 2024. https://www.bestcolleges.com/news/these-colleges-just-banned-tiktok.

Christakis, Erika. "The Dangers of Distracted Parenting: When It Comes to Children's Development, Parents Should Worry Less About Kids' Screen Time-and More About Their Own." *Atlantic*, July/August 2018. https://www.theatlantic.com/amp/article/561752/?__twitter_impression=true.

CIBC. "CIBC Poll: Checked Your Smartphone Recently? Canadian Smartphone Owners Say They Check Their Mobile Device Every Ten Minutes on Average." *PR Newswire*, February 4, 2014. https://www.prnewswire.com/news-releases/cibc-poll-checked-your-smartphone-recently-canadian-smartphone-owners-say-they-check-their-mobile-device-every-10-minutes-on-average-513665311.html.

Clark, Travis. "Netflix Says Its Subscribers Watch an Average of Two Hours a Day—Here's How That Compares with TV Viewing." *Business Insider*, March 13, 2019. https://www.businessinsider.com/netflix-viewing-compared-to-average-tv-viewing-nielsen-chart-2019-3.

Coaston, Jane. "The Facebook Free Speech Battle, Explained." *Vox*, May 6, 2019. https://www.vox.com/technology/2019/5/6/18528250/facebook-speech-conservatives-trump-platform-publisher.

Coughlan, Sean. "Most Children Sleep with Mobile Phone Beside Bed." *BBC News*, January 30, 2020. https://www.bbc.com/news/education-51296197.

Cox, Kate. "Proposed Bill Would End 'Likes' for Young Teens' Online Content." *Ars Technica*, May 3, 2020. https://arstechnica.com/tech-policy/2020/03/proposed-bill-seeks-to-limit-social-media-exploitation-of-kids-under-16.

Coyne, Sarah M. "What Families Should Know About Video Game Addiction." *Institute for Family Studies* (blog), November 20, 2019. https://ifstudies.org/blog/what-families-should-know-about-video-game-addiction.

Croch, Andy. "The Gospel of Steve Jobs." *Christianity Today*, January 21, 2011. http://www.christianitytoday.com/ct/2011/januaryweb-only/gospelstevejobs.html.

———. "The Return of Shame." *Christianity Today*, March 10, 2015. https://www.christianitytoday.com/ct/2015/march/andy-crouch-gospel-in-age-of-public-shame.html.

———. "Steve Jobs: The Secular Prophet." *Wall Street Journal*, October 8, 2011. https://www.wsj.com/articles/SB10001424052970203476804576615403028127550.

———. *The Tech-Wise Family: Everyday Steps for Putting Technology in Its Proper Place*. Grand Rapids: Baker, 2017.

Crouch, Amy, and Andy Crouch. *My Tech-Wise Life: Growing Up and Making Choices in a World of Devices*. Grand Rapids: Baker, 2020.

Davies, William. *This Is Not Normal: The Collapse of Liberal Britain*. New York: Verso, 2020.

DeFrank, Molly. *Digital Detox: The Two-Week Tech Reset For Kids*. Grand Rapids: Baker, 2022.

BIBLIOGRAPHY

Detweiler, Craig. *iGods: How Technology Shapes Our Spiritual and Social Lives*. Grand Rapids: Brazos, 2013.

"Developmental Assets Framework." *Search Institute*, n.d. https://searchinstitute.org/resources-hub/developmental-assets-framework.

Dishman, Lydia. "Meet The Woman Who Combined Neuroscience Tech and Mindfulness." *Fast Company*, March 5, 2015. https://www.fastcompany.com/3043094/meet-the-woman-who-combined-neuroscience-tech-and-mindfulness.

Dixon, Stacy Jo. "Canada Social Media Usage Frequency 2018." *Statista*, August 8, 2019. https://www.statista.com/statistics/553638/social-media-usage-frequency-canada.

———. "Daily Time Spent on Social Networking by Internet Users Worldwide from 2012 to 2024." *Statista*, April 10, 2024. https://www.statista.com/statistics/433871/daily-social-media-usage-worldwide.

Dizikes, Peter. "On Twitter, Falsehood Spreads Faster than Truth." *Economist*, May 10, 2018. https://www.economist.com/science-and-technology/2018/03/10/on-twitter-falsehood-spreads-faster-than-truth.

Dore, Madeleine. "Is There an Upside to Having No Social Life?" *BBC News*, October 12, 2017. http://www.bbc.com/capital/story/20171011-is-there-an-upside-to-having-no-social-life.

Drescher, Elizabeth. *Tweet If You Heart Jesus: Practicing Church in the Digital Reformation*. Harrisburg, PA: Morehouse, 2011.

Drescher, Elizabeth, and Keith Anderson. *Click 2 Save: The Digital Ministry Bible*. Harrisburg, PA: Morehouse, 2012.

Dubois, Elizabeth, et al. "Social Media and Political Engagement in Canada." *Borealis*, December 12, 2018. https://doi.org/10.5683/SP2/9MCJJH.

Dyer, John. *From the Garden to the City: The Redeeming and Corrupting Power of Technology*. Grand Rapids: Kregel, 2022.

"Early Facebook Backer Says Company Uses Methods of Nazi Germany & Goebbels to Addict You." *Edmonton Journal*, November 11, 2017. https://edmontonjournal.com/news/world/early-facebook-backer-says-company-uses-methods-of-nazi-germanys-goebbels-to-addict-you.

Ellul, Jacques. *The Humiliation Of The Word*. Grand Rapids: Eerdmans, 1985.

Elwell, Walter A., ed. *Baker Encyclopedia of the Bible*. 2 vols. Grand Rapids: Baker, 1988.

Freeman, Joshua. "Video Shows Moment Paramedics Helped Victim of CNE's Polar Express Ride Incident." *CTV News*, August 29, 2023. https://toronto.ctvnews.ca/video-shows-moment-paramedics-helped-victim-of-cne-s-polar-express-ride-incident-1.6539204.

Freitas, Donna. *The Happiness Effect: How Social Media Is Driving a Generation to Appear Perfect at Any Cost*. Oxford: Oxford University Press, 2017.

Frey, Jessica, et al. "TikTok Tourette's: Are We Witnessing a Ride in Functional Tic-Like Behavior Driven by Adolescent Social Media Use?" *Psychology Research and Behavior Management* 15 (2022) 3575–85. https://www.ncbi.nlm.nih.gov/pmc/articles/PMC9733629.

Gabruch, Andy. "Infobesity: How Does Information Overload From Digital Technologies Affect Our Relationship With Jesus." DMin thesis, George Fox University, 2023. https://digitalcommons.georgefox.edu/dmin/587.

Gandolf, Stewart. "24/7 Dependence: I'll Bet Your Smartphone Is Within Arm's Reach Right Now." *Healthcare Success* (blog), May 2013. https://healthcaresuccess.com/blog/healthcare-marketing/247-dependence-ill-bet-your-smartphone-is-within-arms-reach-right-now.html.

BIBLIOGRAPHY

Garland, D. E. *Mark*. Grand Rapids: Zondervan, 1996.

Gerson, Jen. "The Greatest Weakness in Western Democracies Is Us." *National Post*, November 12, 2017. http://nationalpost.com/news/world/jen-gerson-the-greatest-weakness-in-western-democracies-is-us.

Gladwell, Malcolm. *The Tipping Point: How Little Things Can Make a Big Difference*. New York: Little, Brown, 2014.

Gorrell, Angela. *Always On: Practicing Faith in a New Media Landscape*. Theology for the Life of the World. Grand Rapids: Baker Academic, 2019.

Greenfield, Adam. *Radical Technologies: The Design of Everyday Life*. New York: Verso, 2018.

———. "A Sociology of the Smartphone." *Longreads* (blog), June 13, 2017. https://longreads.com/2017/06/13/a-sociology-of-the-smartphone.

Grudz, Anatoliy, et al. "Social Media Privacy in Canada." *Ryerson University Social Media Lab*, June 1, 2018. https://doi.org/10.5683/SP/JVOToS.

———. "The State of Social Media in Canada 2017." *Ryerson University Social Media Lab*, February 25, 2018. https://doi.org/10.5683/SP/AL8Z6R.

Güell, Oriol. "Rise of Selfie Deaths Leads Experts to Talk About a Public Health Problem." *El País*, October 29, 2021. https://english.elpais.com/usa/2021-10-29/rise-of-selfie-deaths-leads-experts-to-talk-about-a-public-health-problem.html.

Haidt, Jonathan, and Tobias Rose-Stockwell. "The Dark Psychology of Social Networks: Why It Feels like Everything Is Going Haywire." *Atlantic*, December 2019. https://www.theatlantic.com/magazine/archive/2019/12/social-media-democracy/600763.

Haidt, Jonathan, et al. "Social Media and Mental Health: A Collaborative Review." Unpublished manuscript, n.d. New York University. https://tinyurl.com/SocialMediaMentalHealthReview.

Hampton, Keith, et al. "Social Media and the 'Spiral of Silence.'" *Pew Research Center*, August 26, 2014. https://www.pewinternet.org/2014/08/26/social-media-and-the-spiral-of-silence.

Haque, Umair. "Facebook's Greatest Weapon: Endless Comparison of Ourselves to Others." *Guardian*, January 20, 2018. http://www.theguardian.com/lifeandstyle/2018/jan/20/facebooks-greatest-weapon-endless-comparison-of-ourselves-to-others.

Hawes, Tanya, et al. "Unique Associations of Social Media Use and Online Appearance Preoccupation with Depression, Anxiety, and Appearance Rejection Sensitivity." *Body Image* 33 (2020) 66–76. https://www.sciencedirect.com/science/article/abs/pii/S1740144519303158?via%3Dihub.

Hawkins, Benjamin. "Nation's Biblical Illiteracy at Root a Matter of the Heart." *Pathway*, January 10, 2023. https://mbcpathway.com/2023/01/10/nations-biblical-illiteracy-at-root-a-matter-of-the-heart.

Hibbs, Shane. *The Hidden Power of Electronic Culture: How Media Shapes Faith, the Gospel, and Church*. Grand Rapids: Zondervan, 2006.

Horwitz, Jeff. "Facebook Says Its Rules Apply to All. Company Documents Reveal a Secret Elite That's Exempt." *Wall Street Journal*, September 13, 2021. https://www.wsj.com/articles/facebook-files-xcheck-zuckerberg-elite-rules-11631541353?mod=article_inline.

Housman, Brian. *Tech Savvy Parenting: Navigating Your Child's Digital Life*. Nashville: Randall, 2014.

Houston, Joel. "Why We Need Church in the Digital Age." *Briercrest* (blog), January 2020. https://www.briercrest.ca/blog/why-we-need-church-in-the-digital-age.

Hunt, Melissa, et al. "No More FOMO: Limiting Social Media Decreases Loneliness and Depression." *Journal of Social and Clinical Psychology* 37.10 (2018) 751–68. https://guilfordjournals.com/doi/10.1521/jscp.2018.37.10.751.

Hutton, Robert, and Giles Turner. "Theresa May Tells Facebook, Twitter to Offer Kids in the UK the Right to Delete Their Information." *Financial Post*, May 12, 2017. http://business.financialpost.com/technology/personal-tech/theresa-may-tells-facebook-twitter-to-offer-kids-in-the-u-k-the-right-to-delete-their-information.

"International Selfie Day." *International Days*, June 22, 2024. https://www.internationaldays.co/item-detail/international-selfie-day-2022/r/recu7KeLyHOxZfDaH.

Jiang, Jingjing. "How Teens and Parents Navigate Screen Time and Device Distractions." *Pew Research Center*, August 22, 2018. http://www.pewinternet.org/2018/08/22/how-teens-and-parents-navigate-screen-time-and-device-distractions.

John, Dan. "The Importance of Knowing You Might Be Wrong." *BBC Reel*, May 14, 2020. https://www.bbc.com/videos/cn09q72dg3v0.

Johnston, Sean F. *Techno-Fixers: Origins and Implications of Technological Faith*. Montreal: McGill-Queen's University Press, 2020.

Jones, Nona. *From Social Media to Social Ministry: A Guide to Digital Discipleship*. Grand Rapids: Zondervan, 2020.

Kallas, Priit. "Top Fifteen Most Popular Social Networking Sites and Apps." *DreamGrow*, February 8, 2018. https://www.dreamgrow.com/top-15-most-popular-social-networking-sites.

Keats, John. *The Collected Poems of John Keats*. Delhi, India: Grapevine, 2023.

Kelly, Brendan. "Hundreds of Quebec Parents Flock to Fortnite Lawsuit." *Montreal Gazette*, October 11, 2019. https://montrealgazette.com/news/local-news/hundreds-of-quebec-parents-flock-to-fortnite-lawsuit.

Khan, Adnan R. "How the Internet May Be Turning Us All into Radicals." *Maclean's*, June 26, 2018. https://www.macleans.ca/society/technology/how-the-internet-may-be-turning-us-all-into-radicals.

Khan, Asaduzzaman, et al. "Dose-Dependent and Joint Associations Between Screen Time, Physical Activity, and Mental Wellbeing in Adolescents: An International Observational Study." *Lancet* 5.10 (2021) 729–38. https://www.thelancet.com/journals/lanchi/article/PIIS2352-4642(21)00200-5/fulltext.

Khazan, Olga. "How to Break the Dangerous Cycle of Loneliness." *Bloomberg CityLab*, April 6, 2017. https://www.citylab.com/navigator/2017/04/how-to-break-the-dangerous-cycle-of-loneliness/522180.

Kinnaman, David, and Mark Mattlock. *Faith for Exiles: Five Ways for a New Generation to Follow Jesus in Digital Babylon*. Grand Rapids: Baker, 2019.

Kleinman, Zoe. "Instagram Influencers: Have We Stopped Believing?" *BBC News*, August 24, 2019. https://www.bbc.com/news/technology-49450655.

Schoedel, William R. *Ignatius of Antioch: A Commentary on the Letters of Ignatius of Antioch*. Edited by Helmut Koester. Philadelphia: Fortress, 1985.

Korte, Martin. "The Impact of the Digital Revolution on Human Brain and Behavior: Where Do We Stand?" *Dialogues in Clinical Neuroscience* 22.2 (2020) 101–11.

Kranz, Jeffrey. "All the 'One Another' Commands in the NT." *OverviewBible.com*, March 9, 2014. https://overviewbible.com/one-another-infographic.

Kreider, Alan. *The Patient Ferment of the Early Church: The Improbable Ride of Christianity in the Roman Empire*. Grand Rapids: Baker Academic, 2016.

Kristof, Nicholas. "We Know the Cure for Loneliness. So Why Do We Suffer?" *New York Times*, September 6, 2023. https://www.nytimes.com/2023/09/06/opinion/loneliness-epidemic-solutions.html?unlocked_article_code=1.QU4.AWkq.CqW_tfQzydOO&smid=url-share.

Kroll, Michele M. "Prolonged Social Isolation and Loneliness are Equivalent to Smoking Fifteen Cigarettes A Day." *University of New Hampshire Extension*, May 2, 2022. https://extension.unh.edu/blog/2022/05/prolonged-social-isolation-loneliness-are-equivalent-smoking-15-cigarettes-day.

Lee, Timothy B. "The Internet's Most Important—and Misunderstood—Law, Explained." *Ars Technica*, October 6, 2020. https://arstechnica.com/tech-policy/2020/06/section-230-the-internet-law-politicians-love-to-hate-explained.

Lehman, Charles Fain. "How Do Teens Feel About Screens?" *Institute for Family Studies* (blog), September 5, 2019. https://ifstudies.org/blog/how-do-teens-feel-about-screens.

Levitin, David. *The Organized Mind: Thinking Straight in an Information Overload World*. Toronto: Penguin, 2014.

———. *Successful Aging: A Neuroscientist Explores the Power and Potential of Our Lives*. Toronto: Penguin, 2020.

Lewis, Bex. "Social Media, Peer Surveillance, Spiritual Formation, and Mission: Practicing Christian Faith in a Surveilled Public Space." *Surveillance & Society* 16.4 (2018) 517–32.

Lima, Cristiano. "A Whistleblower's Power: Key Takeaways from the Facebook Papers." *Washington Post*, October 26, 2021. https://www.washingtonpost.com/technology/2021/10/25/what-are-the-facebook-papers.

Little, Becky. "Five Ways Christianity Spread Through Ancient Rome." *History.com*, August 6, 2024. https://www.history.com/news/5-ways-christianity-spread-through-ancient-rome.

Louw, J. P., and E. A. Nida. *Greek-English Lexicon of the New Testament: Based on Semantic Domains*. Electronic ed. of the 2nd ed. 2 vols. New York: United Bible Societies, 1996.

Madigan, Sheri, et al. "Prevalence of Multiple Forms of Sexting Behavior Among Youth: A Systematic Review and Meta-Analysis." *JAMA Pediatrics* 172.4 (2018) 327–35. https://doi.org/10.1001/jamapediatrics.2017.5314.

Madrigal, Alexis C. "The Huge Trend That Realigned the Media Industry Is Over." *Atlantic*, June 13, 2019. https://www.theatlantic.com/technology/archive/2019/06/massive-trend-drove-digital-media-over/591520.

———. "Why No One Answers Their Phone Anymore." *Atlantic*, May 31, 2018. https://www.theatlantic.com/amp/article/561545.

Madu, Zito. "The Important Questions: Why You Should Never Follow the Person You're Dating on Social Media." *National Post*, June 14, 2017. https://nationalpost.com/life/the-important-questions-why-you-should-never-follow-the-person-youre-dating-on-social-media.

Mander, Jason. "Internet Users Have Average of Seven Social Accounts." *GlobalWebIndex* (blog), June 9, 2016. https://blog.globalwebindex.net/chart-of-the-day/internet-users-have-average-of-7-social-accounts.

McClure, Paul K. "Tinkering with Technology and Religion in the Digital Age: The Effects of Internet Use on Religious Belief, Behavior, and Belonging." *Journal for the Scientific Study of Religion* 56.3 (2017) 481–97.

McCracken, Brent. *The Wisdom Pyramid: Feeding Your Soul in a Post-Truth World*. Wheaton, IL: Crossway, 2021.

McGonigal, Jane. *Reality Is Broken: Why Games Make Us Better and How They Can Change the World.* New York: Penguin, 2011.
McKinnon, Melody. "2018 Report: Canadian Social Media Use Statistics." *Online Business Canada*, March 1, 2018. https://canadiansinternet.com/2018-report-canadian-social-media-use-statistics.
———. "2019 Report: Social Media Use in Canada." *Online Business Canada*, June 30, 2019. https://canadiansinternet.com/2019-report-social-media-use-canada.
McLuhan, Marshal. *Understanding Media: The Extension of Man.* 2nd ed. New York: McGraw-Hill, 1964.
McMullan, Thomas. "What Does the Panopticon Mean in the Age of Digital Surveillance?" *Guardian*, July 23, 2015. https://www.theguardian.com/technology/2015/jul/23/panopticon-digital-surveillance-jeremy-bentham.
Meadows, Austin. "Netflix Users Collectively Stream 164.8 Million Hours of Video Per Day." *Streaming Observer* (blog), April 2, 2019. https://www.streamingobserver.com/netflix-users-stream-164-million-hours-per-day.
Meisenzahl, Mary. "Teens Keep Outsmarting Apple's Features for Limiting Screen Time, and Parents Are Starting to Get Frustrated." *Business Insider*, October 19, 2019. https://www.businessinsider.com/apple-screen-time-feature-outsmarted-by-teens-2019-10.
Meurisse, Thibaut. *Master Your Emotions: A Practical Guide to Overcome Negativity and Better Manage your Emotions.* n.p., 2018.
Molitorisz, Sacha. *Net Privacy: How We Can Be Free in an Age of Surveillance.* Toronto: McGill-Queens University Press, 2020.
Moran, Gwen. "This Is How You Future-Proof Your Brain Against Increasing Distractions." *Fast Company*, January 20, 2017. https://www.fastcompany.com/3067233/this-is-how-you-future-proof-your-brain-against-increasing-distractions.
Morris, Leon. *The Gospel According to John.* Revised ed. New International Commentary on the New Testament. Grand Rapids: Eerdmans, 1995.
Murphy, Kate. *You're Not Listening: What You're Missing and Why It Matters.* New York: Celadon, 2021.
Nafousi, Roxie. "International Women's Day: Roxie Nafousi Tries Posting 'Less-Than-Perfect' Images." *BBC News Magazine*, March 8, 2017. http://www.bbc.com/news/magazine-39154628.
Newport, Cal. *Deep Work: Rules for Focused Success in a Distracted World.* New York: Grand Central, 2016.
Newton, Casey, et al. "The Verge Tech Survey: How Americans Really Feel About Facebook, Apple, and More." *Verge*, October 27, 2017. https://www.theverge.com/2017/10/27/16550640/verge-tech-survey-amazon-facebook-google-twitter-popularity.
Nguyen, Lisa. "Fifteen People Who Have Died Playing Video Games." *Gamer*, July 27, 2017. https://www.thegamer.com/15-people-who-have-died-playing-video-games.
Odell, Jenny. *How to Do Nothing: Resisting the Attention Economy.* New York: Melville, 2019.
Office of the Surgeon General (OSG). *Our Epidemic of Loneliness and Isolation: The US Surgeon General's Advisory on the Healing Effects of Social Connection and Community.* Washington, DC: US Department of Health and Human Services, 2023. https://www.hhs.gov/sites/default/files/surgeon-general-social-connection-advisory.pdf.

BIBLIOGRAPHY

Ohlheiser, Abby. "No, the Shark Picture Isn't Real: A Running List of Harvey's Viral Hoaxes." *Washington Post*, August 29, 2017. https://www.washingtonpost.com/news/the-intersect/wp/2017/08/28/no-the-shark-picture-isnt-real-a-running-list-of-harveys-viral-hoaxes.

Olmstead, Kenneth. "A Third of Americans Live in a Household with Three or More Smartphones." *Pew Research Center*, May 25, 2017. http://www.pewresearch.org/fact-tank/2017/05/25/a-third-of-americans-live-in-a-household-with-three-or-more-smartphones.

Orben, Amy, et al. "Social Media's Enduring Effect on Adolescent Life Satisfaction." *Proceedings of the National Academy of Science* 116.21 (2019) 10226–28.

Orlowski, Jeff, dir. *The Social Dilemma*. Los Angeles: Exposure Labs, 2020.

Paulus, Martin P., et al. "Screen Media Activity and Brain Structure in Youth: Evidence for Diverse Structural Correlation Networks from the ABCD Study." *NeuroImage* 185 (2019) 140–53. https://doi.org/10.1016/j.neuroimage.2018.10.040.

Perrin, Andrew. "Americans Are Changing Their Relationship with Facebook." *Pew Research Center*, September 5, 2018. http://www.pewresearch.org/fact-tank/2018/09/05/americans-are-changing-their-relationship-with-facebook.

Peterson, E. H. *The Message: The Bible in Contemporary Language*. Colorado Springs: Nav, 2005.

Peterson, Jordan. "The Deepfake Artists Must Be Stopped Before We No Longer Know What's Real." *National Post*, August 23, 2019. https://nationalpost.com/opinion/jordan-peterson-deep-fake.

"Physical Activity and Screen Time Among Canadian Children and Youth, 2016 and 2017." *Statistics Canada*, April 17, 2019. https://www150.statcan.gc.ca/n1/pub/82-625-x/2019001/article/00003-eng.htm.

Plato. *Phaedrus and the Seventh and Eighth Letters*. Translated by Walter Hamilton. New York: Penguin, 1973.

Pollara Strategic Insights. "SOCIALscape: Canada's Definitive Measurement of Social Media and Messaging Platform Usage Patterns." June 2018. https://www.pollara.com/wp-content/uploads/2017/12/Pollara-SOCIALscape-2018June-Rpt.pdf.

Polyphonic Films. "Why People Are Choosing to Quit Social Media." *BBC Ideas*, May 15, 2020. https:// www.youtube.com/watch?v=ij_xXZAhJPs.

Porges, Seth. "The Futurist: We Predict the iPhone Will Bomb." *TechCrunch*, June 7, 2007. http://social.techcrunch.com/2007/06/07/the-futurist-we-predict-the-iphone-will-bomb.

"A Portrait of Canadian Youth." *Statistics Canada*, February 7, 2018. https://www150.statcan.gc.ca/n1/pub/11-631-x/11-631-x2018001-eng.htm.

Powers, Neil. "Half of Young Canadian Adults Spend Two or More Hours per Day on Their Cellphones." *Financial Post*, February 24, 2018. https://business.financialpost.com/telecom/half-of-young-canadian-adults-spend-two-or-more-hours-per-day-on-their-cellphones.

Przybylski, Andrew K., and Netta Weinstein. "A Large-Scale Test of the Goldilocks Hypothesis: Quantifying the Relations Between Digital-Screen Use and the Mental Well-Being of Adolescents." *Psychological Science* 28.2 (2017) 204–15. https://journals.sagepub.com/doi/full/10.1177/0956797616678438.

Pushter, Jacob, et al. "Social Media Use Continues to Rise in Developing Countries but Plateaus Across Developed Ones: Digital Divides Remain, Both Within and Across Countries." *Pew Research Center*, June 19, 2018. http://assets.pewresearch.org/wp-content/uploads/sites/2/2018/06/15135408/Pew-Research-Center_Global-Tech-Social-Media-Use_2018.06.19.pdf.

Qureshi, Usman. "Reddit Users Are Angry iPhone XS Selfies Are Too Beautiful." *iPhone in Canada*, September 26, 2018. https://www.iphoneincanada.ca/news/iphone-xs-selfies-are-too-beautiful.

Rainie, Lee, and Barry Wellman. *Networked: The New Social Operating System*. Reprint, Cambridge, MA: MIT Press, 2014.

Rapee, Ronald M., et al. "Risk for Social Anxiety in Early Adolescence: Longitudinal Impact of Pubertal Development, Appearance Comparisons, and Peer Connections." *Behaviour Research and Therapy* 154.1 (2022) 104126.

Reinink, Jonathan. "How Software Is Helping Churches Stay Connected." *Challies*, October 7, 2019. https://www.challies.com/sponsored/how-software-is-helping-churches-stay-connected.

Reinke, Tony. *Twelve Ways Your Phone Is Changing You*. Wheaton: Crossway, 2017.

Rideout, Victoria. *The Common Sense Census: Media Use by Kids Age Zero to Eight*. San Francisco: Common Sense, 2017. https://www.commonsensemedia.org/sites/default/files/research/report/csm_zerotoeight_fullreport_release_2.pdf.

Rideout, Victoria, et al. *Coping with COVID-19: How Young People Use Digital Media to Manage Their Mental Health*. San Francisco: Common Sense, 2021. https://www.commonsensemedia.org/sites/default/files/research/report/2021-coping-with-covid19-full-report.pdf.

Rideout, Victoria, and Michael B. Robb. *Social Media, Social Life: Teens Reveal Their Experiences*. San Francisco: Common Sense, 2018. https://www.commonsensemedia.org/sites/default/files/uploads/research/2018_cs_socialmediasociallife_fullreport-final-release_2_lowres.pdf.

Rinaldi, Luc. "They Lost their Kids to *Fortnite*." *Maclean's*, July 13, 2023. https://macleans.ca/longforms/fortnite-addiction-video-games-mental-health.

Roderique, Hadiya. "I Have 1,605 Facebook Friends. Why Do I Feel So Alone?" *National Post*, February 14, 2018. http://nationalpost.com/feature/i-have-1605-facebook-friends-why-do-i-feel-so-alone.

Rosoff, Matt. "Facebook Exodus: Nearly Half of Young Users Have Deleted the App from Their Phone in the Last Year, Says Study." *CNBC*, September 5, 2018. https://www.cnbc.com/2018/09/05/facebook-exodus-44-percent-of-americans-age-18-29-have-deleted-app.html.

Routledge, Clay. "What Are the Social and Psychological Costs of Our Computer-Mediated Lives?" *Institute for Family Studies* (blog), August 15, 2019. https://ifstudies.org/blog/what-are-the-social-and-psychological-costs-of-our-computer-mediated-lives.

Rudd, Steven. "The Exodus Route: Travel Times, Distances, Rates of Travel, Days of the Week." *Bible.ca*, May 2020. https://www.bible.ca/archeology/bible-archeology-exodus-route-travel-times-distances-days.htm.

Russon, Mary-Ann. "Are You Able to Switch off When on Holiday?" *BBC News*, August 9, 2019. https://www.bbc.com/news/business-49234310.

Sacasas, L. M. "A Theory of Zoom Fatigue." *Convivial Society* (blog), April 20, 2020. https://theconvivialsociety.substack.com/p/a-theory-of-zoom-fatigue.

Satariano, Adam, and Selina Wang. "'The Only Electricity We Use Is One Lamp': Apple Execs, Facebook Billionaires Embrace Tech Diets for Devices, Services They Helped Create." *National Post*, February 5, 2018. http://nationalpost.com/technology/the-only-electricity-we-use-is-one-lamp-apple-execs-facebook-billionaires-embrace-tech-diets-for-devices-services-they-helped-create/wcm/bfa17b88-94ad-4294-8f3b-4ffe6646dbaa.

Sax, Leonard. "How Social Media May Harm Boys and Girls Differently." *Psychology Today*, May 12, 2020. https://www.psychologytoday.com/blog/sax-sex/202005/how-social-media-harms-boys-and-girls-differently.

Schaefer Riley, Naomi. "If We're Concerned About Harmful Media Content, We Should Limit Kids' Screen Time." *Institute for Family Studies* (blog), August 1, 2019. https://ifstudies.org/blog/if-were-concerned-about-harmful-media-content-we-should-limit-kids-screen-time.

Schaeffer, Katherine. "Five Facts About How Americans Use Facebook, Two Decades After Its Launch." *Pew Research Center*, February 2, 2024. https://www.pewresearch.org/short-reads/2024/02/02/5-facts-about-how-americans-use-facebook-two-decades-after-its-launch.

Schwartz, D. R. "Pontius Pilate (Person)." In *The Anchor Yale Bible Dictionary*, edited by David Noel Freedman, 5:399. New York: Doubleday, 1992.

Schultze, Quentin J. *Habits of the High-Tech Heart: Living Virtuously in the Information Age*. Grand Rapids: Baker Academic, 2002.

Shankar, Bradly. "Canadians Watch More Netflix During Weekends than the Average Global User." *MobileSyrup*, March 10, 2018. https://mobilesyrup.com/2018/03/10/canada-netflix-weekend-usage-global-averages.

Sherwood, Ben. "Leading and Succeeding in the Age of Disruption." *Global Leadership Network*, August 8, 2019. https://globalleadership.org/articles/leading-organizations/ben-sherwood-leading-and-succeeding-in-the-age-of-disruption.

Silverman, Ellie. "Facebook's First President, on Facebook: 'God Only Knows What It's Doing to Our Children's Brains.'" *Washington Post*, November 9, 2024. https://www.washingtonpost.com/news/the-switch/wp/2017/11/09/facebooks-first-president-on-facebook-god-only-knows-what-its-doing-to-our-childrens-brains.

Sittser, Gerald L. *Resilient Faith: How the Early Christian "Third Way" Changed the World*. Grand Rapids: Brazos, 2019.

"Smartphone Screen Time: Baby Boomers and Millennials." *Provision Living* (blog), March 1, 2019. https://www.provisionliving.com/blog/smartphone-screen-time-baby-boomers-and-millennials.

Smith, Aaron, and Monica Anderson. "Automation in Everyday Life." *Pew Research Center*, October 4, 2017. https://www.pewresearch.org/internet/2017/10/04/automation-in-everyday-life.

———. "Social Media Use in 2018." *Pew Research Center*, March 1, 2018. http://assets.pewresearch.org/wp-content/uploads/sites/14/2018/03/01105133/PI_2018.03.01_Social-Media_FINAL.pdf.

Smith, Collin. "Jesus Answers All His People's Questions." *Open the Bible* (blog), February 3, 2008. https://openthebible.org/sermon/jesus-answers-all-questions.

Smith, Kit. "105 Amazing Social Media Statistics and Facts." *Brandwatch*, November 18, 2017. https://www.brandwatch.com/blog/96-amazing-social-media-statistics-and-facts-for-2016.

"Social Media's Role in Reshaping Power in Politics." *Maclean's*, March 12, 2019. https://www.macleans.ca/opinion/snc-lavalin-scandal-social-media-power-politics.

Sood, Ashvin. "How to Counter TikTok's Mental Health Misinformation." *Psychology Today*, February 1, 2023. https://www.psychologytoday.com/us/blog/psychiatrys-think-tank/202301/how-to-counter-tiktoks-mental-health-misinformation.
Stahl, William A. *God and the Chip: Religion and the Culture of Technology*. Waterloo, ON: Wilfred Laurier University Press, 1999.
Stoddart, Eric. "The Internet Gaze." In *The HTML of Cruciform Love: Toward a Theology of the Internet*, edited by John Frederick and Eric Lewellen, 117–31. Eugene, OR: Wipf & Stock, 2019.
Strange, J. F. "Nazareth (Place)." In *The Anchor Yale Bible Dictionary*, edited by David Noel Freedman, 4:1050. New York: Doubleday, 1992.
Sullivan, Bob, and Hugh Thompson. "A Focus on Distraction." *New York Times*, May 3, 2013. http://www.nytimes.com/2013/05/05/opinion/sunday/a-focus-on-distraction.html.
Sweat, Becky. "How Can You Deal With Information Overload?" *Beyond Today*, August 1, 2010. https://www.ucg.org/the-good-news/how-can-you-deal-with-information-overload.
Sweet, Len. *Giving Blood: A Fresh Paradigm to Preaching*. Grand Rapids: Zondervan, 2014.
Thompson, Allan, ed. *Media and Mass Atrocity: The Rwanda Genocide and Beyond*. Montreal: McGill-Queen's University Press, 2019.
Thompson, Clive. *Coders: The Making of a New Tribe and the Remaking of the World*. New York: Penguin, 2019.
Tilford, Ashlee. "Survey: 78 Percent of Pet Owners Acquired Pets During Pandemic." *Forbes Advisor*, April 10, 2022. https://www.forbes.com/advisor/pet-insurance/survey-78-pet-owners-acquired-pets-during-pandemic.
Trenqualye, Madeleine de. "Alone in a Crowded City." *University of British Columbia Magazine*, June 8, 2022. https://magazine.alumni.ubc.ca/2022/spring-2022/health-humanities/alone-crowded-city.
Triggle, Nick. "Is Social Media to Thank for Low Teen Pregnancy Rates?" *BBC News*, March 27, 2018. https://www.bbc.com/news/health-43506784.
Twenge, Jean M. "Have Smartphones Destroyed a Generation?" *Atlantic*, August 3, 2017. https://www.theatlantic.com/amp/article/534198.
———. *iGen: Why Today's Super-Connected Kids Are Growing Up Less Rebellious, More Tolerant, Less Happy—and Completely Unprepared for Adulthood—and What That Means for the Rest of Us*. New York: Atria, 2017.
———. "The Mental Health Crisis Among America's Youth Is Real—and Staggering." *Institute for Family Studies* (blog), March 18, 2019. https://ifstudies.org/blog/the-mental-health-crisis-among-americas-youth-is-realand-staggering.
———. "Steve Jobs, Apple and Social Anxiety: The iPhone's Birthday is Nothing to Celebrate." *Newsweek*, July 1, 2017. http://www.newsweek.com/steve-jobs-apple-and-social-anxiety-iphones-birthday-nothing-celebrate-630416.
Twenge, Jean M., et al. "Underestimating Digital Media Harm." *Nature Human Behaviour* 4.4 (2020) 346–48. https://doi.org/10.1038/s41562-020-0839-4.
Vaughan, Michael. "Know Your Limits, Your Brain Can Only Take So Much." *Entrepreneur*, January 21, 2014. https://www.entrepreneur.com/living/know-your-limits-your-brain-can-only-take-so-much/230925.
Vega, Nicolas. "Sean Parker on Facebook: We Created a Monster." *New York Post*, November 9, 2017. https://nypost.com/2017/11/09/sean-parker-on-facebook-we-created-a-monster.

Vogels, Emily A. "Millennials Stand Out for Their Technology Use, but Older Generations Also Embrace Digital Life." *Pew Research Center*, September 9, 2019. https://www.pewresearch.org/short-reads/2019/09/09/us-generations-technology-use.

Wallen, Jack. "The Rise of the Linux Distribution-Specific Laptop." *TechRepublic*, March 9, 2020. https://www.techrepublic.com/article/the-rise-of-the-linux-distribution-specific-laptop.

"What Is Chronic Loneliness and How Can We Stay Connected?" *Relationships Australia New South Wales (ANSW)* (blog), October 24, 2023. https://www.relationshipsnsw.org.au/blog/chronic-loneliness-stay-connected.

"What's Behind 'Shocking' US Life Expectancy Decline—and What to Do About It." *Harvard T. H. Chan School of Public Health*, April 13, 2023. https://www.hsph.harvard.edu/news/hsph-in-the-news/whats-behind-shocking-u-s-life-expectancy-decline-and-what-to-do-about-it.

"Why Tic-Like Behaviors Are on the Rise in Children and Teens." *Science of Health* (blog), March 25, 2024. https://www.uhhospitals.org/blog/articles/2024/03/why-tic-like-behaviors-are-on-the-rise-in-children-and-teens.

Winnick, Michael. "Putting a Finger on Our Phone Obsession." *People Nerds*, June 16, 2017. https://dscout.com/people-nerds/mobile-touches.

Wojcik, Stefan, and Adam Hughes. "Sizing Up Twitter Users." *Pew Research Center*, April 24, 2019. https://www.pewinternet.org/2019/04/24/sizing-up-twitter-users.

Woolley, Paul. "Questions Jesus Asked: The Power of the Question." *London Institute for Contemporary Christianity*, November 1, 2021. https://licc.org.uk/resources/questions-jesus-asked-the-power-of-the-question.

World Health Organization (WHO), Regional Office for the Eastern Mediterranean. "Excessive Screen Use and Gaming Considerations During #COVID19." 2020. https://iris.who.int/handle/10665/333467.

Wright, H. Norman. *A Better Way to Think: Using Positive Thoughts to Change Your Life*. Grand Rapids: Revell, 2011.

www.ingramcontent.com/pod-product-compliance
Lightning Source LLC
Chambersburg PA
CBHW031355230426
43670CB00006B/551